D0223745

GENESIS: HISTORY, FICTION, or NEITHER?

THREE
VIEWS   **THE BIBLE'S EARLIEST CHAPTERS**
ON

Books in the Counterpoints Series

Bible and Theology

Five Views on Biblical Inerrancy

Five Views on Law and Gospel

Four Views on Divine Providence

Four Views on Hell

Four Views on Moving beyond the Bible to Theology

Four Views on the Apostle Paul

Four Views on the Book of Revelation

Four Views on the Historical Adam

Show Them No Mercy

Three Views on Creation and Evolution

Three Views on the Millennium and Beyond

Three Views on the New Testament Use of the Old Testament

Two Views on the Doctrine of the Trinity

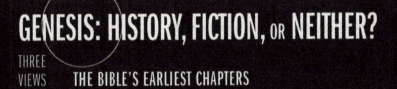

GENESIS: HISTORY, FICTION, OR NEITHER?

THREE VIEWS ON THE BIBLE'S EARLIEST CHAPTERS

James K. Hoffmeier

Gordon J. Wenham

Kenton L. Sparks

Charles Halton, general editor
Stanley N. Gundry, series editor

COUNTERPOINTS
BIBLE & THEOLOGY

ZONDERVAN

Genesis: History, Fiction, or Neither?
Copyright © 2015 by Charles Halton, James K. Hoffmeier, Gordon J. Wenham, Kenton
L. Sparks

This title is also available as a Zondervan ebook. Visit www.zondervan.com/ebooks.

Requests for information should be addressed to:
Zondervan, 3900 Sparks Dr. SE, Grand Rapids, Michigan 49546

Library of Congress Cataloging-in-Publication Data

Halton, Charles, 1978-
        Genesis : history, fiction, or neither : three views on the Bible's earliest
    chapters / Charles Halton, general editor ; James K. Hoffmeier, Gordon J. Wenham,
    Kenton L. Sparks.
            pages cm. — (Counterpoints: Bible and theology)
        Includes index.
        ISBN 978-0-310-51494-7 (softcover)
        1. Bible. Genesis, I-XI — Criticism, interpretation, etc. I. Halton, Charles,
    1978- editor. II. Title.
    BS1235.52.H65 2015
    222'.1106 — dc23   2014030320

Cover design: Tammy Johnson
Cover photography: Corbis Images
Interior design: Matthew Van Zomeran

Printed in the United States of America

HB 08.18.2021

To those who, like Jacob,
wrestle with God and man.

CONTENTS

Contributors 9

Abbreviations 11

INTRODUCTION

A DESICCATED FINGER AND THE STUDY OF GENRE 13
CHARLES HALTON

1. **GENESIS 1 - 11 AS HISTORY AND THEOLOGY** 23
   JAMES K. HOFFMEIER

   ### Responses

   GORDON J. WENHAM 59
   KENTON L. SPARKS 63

2. **GENESIS 1 - 11 AS PROTOHISTORY** 73
   GORDON J. WENHAM

   ### Responses

   JAMES K. HOFFMEIER 98
   KENTON L. SPARKS 101

3. **GENESIS 1 - 11 AS ANCIENT HISTORIOGRAPHY** 110
   KENTON L. SPARKS

   ### Responses

   JAMES K. HOFFMEIER 140
   GORDON J. WENHAM 150

CONCLUSION

WE DISAGREE. WHAT NOW? 155

CHARLES HALTON

Scripture Index 164
Subject Index 167

CONTRIBUTORS

Charles Halton (PhD, Hebrew Union College-Jewish Institute of Religion) is assistant professor in theology at Houston Baptist University. He has contributed to *The IVP Dictionary of the Old Testament: Prophets* and *Reading Akkadian Prayers and Hymns: An Introduction*. He is the co-author of *The First Female Authors: An Anthology of Women's Writing in Mesopotamia*. He virtually resides at charleshalton.com and his physical residence is in Louisville, Kentucky.

James K. Hoffmeier (PhD, University of Toronto) is professor of Old Testament and Near Eastern archaeology at Trinity International University Divinity School in Deerfield, Illinois. He is the author of *Ancient Israel in Sinai* and *Israel in Egypt*, and co-author of *Faith, Tradition and History*.

Gordon J. Wenham (PhD, University of London) is tutor in Old Testament at Trinity College, Bristol, England, and professor emeritus of Old Testament at the University of Gloucestershire. He is the author or editor of numerous books, including *Story as Torah* and commentaries on Genesis, Leviticus, and Numbers.

Kenton L. Sparks (Ph.D., University of North Carolina) is professor of biblical studies and vice president for enrollment management at Eastern University. He is the author of several books, including *Ancient Texts for the Study of the Hebrew Bible*, *God's Word in Human Words*, and *Sacred Word, Broken Word*.

ABREVIATIONS

ABD   *Anchor Bible Dictionary.* Edited by David Noel Freedman.
             6 vols. New York: Doubleday, 1992
AnBib   Analecta biblica
ANET   *Ancient Near Eastern Texts Relating to the Old Testament.*
             Edited by James B. Pritchard. 3d ed. Princeton:
             Princeton University Press, 1969
ATSHB   *Ancient Texts for the Study of the Hebrew Bible.* Kenton Sparks.
             Grand Rapids: Baker, 2005
BASOR   *Bulletin of the American Schools of Oriental Research*
BJRL   *Bulletin of the John Rylands University Library of Manchester*
BMes   Bibliotheca Mesopotamica
CHANE   *Culture and History of the Ancient Near East*
COS   *The Context of Scripture.* Edited by William W. Hallo. 3 vols.
             Leiden: Brill, 1997–2002
JANES   *Journal of the Ancient Near Eastern Society*
JBL   *Journal of Biblical Literature*
JBR   *Journal of Bible and Religion*
JNES   *Journal of Near Eastern Studies*
JSOT   *Journal for the Study of the Old Testament*
JSOTSup   Journal for the Study of the Old Testament Supplement Series
JSSEA   *Journal of the Society for the Study of Egyptian Antiquities*
KBL   Koehler, Ludwig, and Walter Baumgartner. *Lexicon in*
             Veteris Testamenti libros. Translated and updated by
             M. E. J. Richardson. Leiden, 2001
OBO   Orbis Biblicus et Orientalis
OEANE   *The Oxford Encyclopedia of Archaeology in the Near East.*
             Edited by Eric M. Meyers. 5 vols. New York:
             Oxford University Press, 1997
OTS   Old Testament Studies
SAAS   State Archives of Assyrian Studies
SANE   Sources of the Ancient Near East

VT   *Vetus Testamentum*
YNER   Yale Near Eastern Researches
ZAW   *Zeitschrift für die alttestamentliche Wissenschaft*

A DESICCATED FINGER AND THE STUDY OF GENRE

"No, no! The adventures first, explanations take such a dreadful time."

Lewis Carroll, *Alice's Adventures in Wonderland & Through the Looking-Glass*

"In our study of antiquity, we are operating with a deficiency as a matter of course because we must work with the remains that are left to us."

Angela R. Roskop, *The Wilderness Itineraries*

They cracked open the coffin and surveyed the shriveled remains, debating the best way to lift them out. They were transferring the body from the place of its hasty internment ninety-five years prior to a glorious tomb in the Basilica of Santa Croce in Florence. The move reflected Galileo Galilei's change in status, once convicted as "vehemently suspect of heresy" and denied a proper burial, he was posthumously pardoned and placed in a tomb near his father. In a moment when no one was looking, a devoted admirer snapped a few fingers off the former heretic. Like pious Christians venerating the Crown of Thorns at Notre-Dame Cathedral, these digits became objects of devotion for those of a more critical bent. The slivers of bone and desiccated flesh changed hands several times until they came to rest in the Museo Galileo on the bank of the Arno. The middle finger now sits alone, on display in a glass egg, pointing upward toward the heavens, as it seems, in perpetual salute to the Catholic Church.

At issue was Galileo's observation that the earth revolves around the sun, an understanding that is universally accepted today but seems to contradict a number of biblical passages. Some Christians, well-meaning and otherwise, brought these verses to Galileo's attention and demanded an explanation. He agreed that passages like 1 Chronicles 16:30b, "The world is firmly established; it cannot be moved," represent a fixed earth.[1] But, he added, the Bible often means "things which are quite different from what its bare words signify." He went on to explain:

> Hence in expounding the Bible if one were always to confine one-self to the unadorned grammatical meaning, one might fall into error ... Thus it would be necessary to assign to God feet, hands, and eyes, as well as corporeal and human affections, such as anger, repentance, hatred, and sometimes even the forgetting of things past and ignorance of those to come. These propositions uttered by the Holy Ghost were set down in that manner by the sacred scribes in order to accommodate them to the capacities of the common people, who are rude and unlearned.[2]

Galileo thought that these passages should be interpreted not accord-ing to their strict, grammatical meaning but according to a different set of rules: rules that take into account the complexities of communication such as metaphor, symbolism, and imagery; and rules that operate at a level higher than the sentence, a sort of macro-syntax. His examiners unanimously disagreed and in 1633 threatened him with torture, banned the sale of his books, and placed him under house arrest for the balance of his life.[3] Three hundred and fifty years later the Catholic Church finally admitted that the logic behind Galileo's conviction (but not the convic-tion itself) was in error when Pope John Paul II spoke to the Pontifical Academy of Sciences on October 31, 1981: "The error of the theologians of the time, when they maintained the centrality of the earth, was to think that our understanding of the physical world's structure was, in some way, imposed by the literal sense of Sacred Scripture."[4]

---

1. Similarly, Pss 93:1, 96:10, 104:5; and Eccl 1:5.

2. From Galileo's "Letter to Madame Christina of Lorraine, Grand Duchess of Tuscany," in *Discoveries and Opinions of Galileo* (trans. Stillman Drake; New York: Doubleday, 1957), 181.

3. Noah J. Efron, "Myth 8. That Galileo Was Imprisoned and Tortured for Advocating Copernicanism" in *Galileo Goes to Jail and Other Myths about Science and Religion* (ed. Ronald L. Numbers; Cambridge, MA: Harvard University Press, 2009), 68–78.

4. The English translation of the Pope's address, given in French, may be found in *L'Osservatore Romano* N. 44 (1264), 4 November 1992.

A Different Set of Rules

Thankfully, the Inquisitions have largely subsided but the issues underlying the Galileo case are still very much in play. Galileo had the courage—or what his inquisitors regarded as hubris—to read the Bible with sensitivity toward its various genres. Though he never used this term, he gave definition to an interpretive technique that all of us employ without thinking. We read Jesus' statement, "I am the true vine, and my Father is the gardener," and no one this side of a sanitarium thinks Jesus believed that leaves sprouted from his side after his father applied a touch of fertilizer. His statement was not a literal description of fact. It describes something different than what its grammar implies; we know this intuitively. But how far do we take this? What other scriptural passages are like this, and, once they are identified, what do we do with them? These are the questions that sent suspects to the rack and continue to preoccupy conscientious interpreters today.

These questions are always in the background whether or not an interpreter is as explicit about them as Galileo. Fundamentally, the process of understanding a text involves two parts: reading and interpreting. Reading is an attempt to understand the connotation of words and their relation to one another. It is the act of decoding the meanings that an author embeds through his or her selection of words, the forms he or she sets them in, and their placement within sentences. For instance, a competent reader of English knows that apple can refer to a Pink Lady or a Golden Delicious but not a pine cone. A competent reader of English also knows that verbs follow the subjects that govern them and words ending in -ly modify actions. A competent reader knows—whether through conscious study or subconscious assimilation—the set of rules that an author used to encode meaning within a string of words. For the act of reading to be successful, both author and reader must share the same code, the same system of representing meaning in graphical form.[5] If an author records her thoughts in Chinese and a reader familiar only with French tries to read them, confusion will result.

The act of reading does not stop when a text is deciphered. Once a text is read, interpretation begins. Even if a reader is able to understand

---

5. Umberto Eco, "Between Author and Text," in *Interpretation and Overinterpretation* (ed. Stefan Collini; Cambridge: Cambridge University Press, 1992), 68.

every word of a sentence along with their functions within it, he or she still must ask the question: "What does this mean?" Many factors go into answering this question but one of the most important is determining the type of text one is reading. A reader approaches a romance novel very differently than the maintenance guide for his or her van. Identical sentences could have vastly different meanings within these books. For a competent reader, this is not a problem. He or she will understand that a wrench means a wrench in a maintenance guide but it could mean something else entirely in a romance novel. He or she knows this because they calibrate their expectations regarding the range of meanings of words based upon the type of text being read. The range of meaning for wrench is quite narrow and technical in an instruction manual. Within romantic fiction, its potential meaning is much wider and could include metaphorical associations. Competent readers know this without thinking.

Competent writers signal the type, or genre, of the texts they pen by adopting commonly accepted forms. Just like the rules of syntax which govern the placement of words within a sentence, clusters of sentences—even those as long as books—have rules as well. For instance, if a text begins with the phrase, "Once upon a time," a competent reader knows that she is reading is a "fairy tale," a short, fictional story which has a happy ending and is intended primarily for young children. That one, little phrase conveys an amazing amount of information. It also indicates the way in which the text should be interpreted. One looks to fairy tales for entertainment and a life lesson but not to recreate historical chronologies.

This is the concept that Galileo was trying to illustrate—that our job as competent students of Scripture does not end when we are able to read its sentences and understand its grammar. We must move on to the task of interpretation and ask, "What does this mean?" The ways in which we answer this question must take into account the type of text we are reading. As Galileo said, there are passages that *demand* that we interpret them differently than their grammar implies.

All of this might seem very straightforward, after all, who doesn't know that a traffic ticket means something different than a love letter? The reason why this is straightforward is because we are familiar with the genres that fill our culture. But what happens when we leave our culture and inhabit a different one, a culture that may or may not have the same rules and expectations that govern its genres, and may even have entirely different genres than those we are familiar with? In order to read these texts competently, we must make explicit what we normally intuit.

The Study of Genre

Interpreters of the Bible have always dealt with genre but for a long time it remained mostly in the background, a concept that was part of the interpretive process but rarely explored in its own right. The study of genre came to the fore after the discovery of ancient Near Eastern texts that bear a remarkable similarity to the Bible. In the nineteenth century, the scholarly world was abuzz over newly discovered Babylonian creation accounts, Assyrian prophecies, and Sumerian king lists. Almost immediately, people began making comparisons between these texts and the themes and forms of Sacred Scripture. Yet, before these discussions could develop too far, another conversation had to take place.

In order for comparisons to be meaningful, there needs to be some point of commonality between the objects under study. On its face, it makes no sense to place a Babylonian creation account next to a biblical law and look for differences.[6] Divergences between these texts may not necessarily reflect the separate cultural traditions and ideological environments in which these documents were written; more likely, variations stem from the different purposes in writing. Comparisons are more meaningful when they involve texts of the same type, law to law and creation account to creation account. In order for scholars to compare newly discovered ancient Near Eastern documents with the Bible, they needed to determine the genres of the various texts.

Hermann Gunkel (1862–1932) is often regarded as the formative voice behind the effort to place the study of genre—or as it is also called, form criticism—within its own area of scholarly study. Gunkel

---

6. I say, "On its face," because there are times when a comparison of texts from different genres yields surprising results. For example, John Walton finds many similarities between Genesis 1 and Mesopotamian temple hymns. See *Genesis One as Ancient Cosmology* (Winona Lake: Eisenbrauns, 2011) and *The Lost World of Genesis One: Ancient Cosmology and the Origins Debate* (Downers Grove: IVP, 2009).

focused mainly on the Bible and identified the genres within it according to three criteria: 1) the mood, or internal disposition of the author; 2) the structure, or form, of the text; and 3) the context or "life setting" (often referred to as *Sitz im Leben* in academic literature). Gunkel's approach was incredibly influential but scholars soon recognized it contained several weaknesses and limitations.[7]

Gunkel had a very rigid conception of genre—a text was one genre and only one genre. Scholars came to understand that writing is more flexible than this. For instance, authors can combine features of several different genres into one. Jonathan Swift did this when he wrote *Gulliver's Travels*. On one hand, it's a children's story filled with tiny peoples and flying islands. On the other, it's a savage attack on the embrace of scientism and overly optimistic views of human nature. Is *Gulliver's Travels* a children's novel, an adult political satire, or a critique of religious ideology? In fact, it's all of these things; no one label adequately describes it. In some sense, every text is like this. Each act of writing combines words and forms in new ways to create texts of their own unique genre.

We might see this as a problem—genres multiplying like rabbits and producing a chaotic mess of a million different and undecipherable documents. In practice, genres don't work this way. Every piece of writing is produced within a particular context and competent writers craft their works so that they are similar enough to existing structures that readers who share the same context can make sense of them. But what about readers from different contexts? These readers may or may not share the same expectations and set of interpretive rules. In many cases, particularly those in which many years and much cultural distance separates author and reader, readers will need to do some work in order to become competent interpreters. In all likelihood, these readers will not have an innate understanding of the genres that ancient authors used since they inhabit a vastly different world. Readers will first need to understand the genre of the text and how it worked within the author's cultural environment before they will be able to successfully address the question: "What does this text mean?" This is the situation that we face

---

7. Kenton L. Sparks, *Ancient Texts for the Study of the Hebrew Bible: A Guide to the Background Literature* (Peabody, MA: Hendrickson, 2005), 1–24.

when we approach Genesis 1–11. This is also why Genesis 1–11 is one of the most controversial parts of the Bible.

Genre and Genesis 1–11

We are thousands of years removed from the origins of the book of Genesis. We live in a world that has sent people to the moon and back, that uses magnets to map the inside of human bodies; we work and sleep in climate controlled buildings, travel in air-conditioned cars, fly in pressurized planes, and send text messages through pieces of metal and glass small enough to slip into the pockets of our pants. The world of Genesis was dusty and barely literate. The people of its time were preoccupied with satiating hunger and securing physical safety. They consulted shamans for toothaches, thought that the gods spoke through birth defects and markings on sheep livers, and they defecated into ditches.[8] Reading Genesis is like traveling from downtown Dublin to rural Angola. The contexts of author and reader could hardly be more different.

To be sure, we don't share the cultural context of the authors of Genesis but we do hold in common the experience of being human — joy at childbirth and mourning at death. We relish a good story just as much as they did. We have unfulfilled dreams, we take pride in accomplishment, and we experience interpersonal strife, just like they did. At the same time as there are vast differences between us, we share with the biblical writers some of life's most fundamental elements. How much of this shared experience translates into our understanding of the literary genres that they used? How big are the gaps in our knowledge?

Is Genesis 1–11 similar to the genres of our culture? If so, what genre is it? Is it factual history, fictional fable, or somewhere in between? And how does its overall genre affect our interpretation of individual

---

8. Deuteronomy 23:12–14 specifies the way in which this was to be done: "Designate a place outside the camp where you can go to relieve yourself. As part of your equipment have something to dig with, and when you relieve yourself, dig a hole and cover up your excrement. For the LORD your God moves about in your camp to protect you and to deliver your enemies to you. Your camp must be holy, so that he will not see among you anything indecent and turn away from you" (NIV). Not everyone believes that rise of modern toilets is a good thing. According to the Spanish cheesemaker, Ambrosio Molinos de las Heras, one of the most satisfying parts of life is squatting in a field with one's friends (Michael Paterniti, *The Telling Room: A Tale of Love, Betrayal, Revenge, and the World's Greatest Piece of Cheese* [New York: Random House, 2013], 43). Maybe the ancients understood the joys of life more deeply than we do?

passages? After two thousand years of study, these questions remain a matter of debate. This book is intended to reflect this debate as well as to help individuals and congregations have a more informed and focused discussion on the topic. The book itself will not arrive at any particular conclusion, although each author advocates for the position that he believes is most beneficial.

The contributors—James Hoffmeier, Gordon Wenham, and Kenton Sparks—were asked to respond to four elements with their essays: 1) identify the genre of Genesis 1–11; 2) explain why this is the genre of Genesis 1–11; 3) explore the implications of this genre designation for biblical interpretation; and 4) apply their approach to the interpretation of three specific passages: the story of the Nephilim (6:1–4), Noah and the ark (6:9–9:26), and the Tower of Babel (11:1–9). In his essay, "Genesis 1–11 as History and Theology," James Hoffmeier argues that the Genesis narrative relates historical facts, real events that happened in space and time. Hoffmeier points to features within Genesis, such as geographical clues and literary elements, that signaled to ancient readers that these stories were to be understood as historical. Gordon Wenham agrees with this to a point. In his essay, "Genesis 1–11 as Protohistory," Wenham sees an undercurrent of history beneath the Genesis account but he likens it to viewing an abstract painting—the picture is there but the details are fuzzy. Wenham believes that Genesis is protohistory, a form of writing that has links to the past but interprets history for the sake of the present. Kenton Sparks explains that the authors of Genesis wrote in typically ancient ways which did not intend to produce history as we know it. In his essay, "Genesis 1–11 as Ancient Historiography," Sparks argues that many of the events recounted in Genesis did not happen as the narrative states. Each author was also asked to provide a brief response to the other.

While the dialog may get spirited at times, its purpose is to expose the strengths and weaknesses of each position. In the spirit of Galileo, all of the contributors agree that competent interpretation of Scripture requires sensitivity to genre. They disagree, however, over the precise nature of the genre of Genesis 1–11 and its implications.

To a large extent, competent reading involves getting to know ourselves as much as it does understanding an author. Christopher Wall observes, "Though reading is a close collaboration between a reader and text, it can only start when you notice the difference between what you see and what you *want* to see."[9] We hope that this conversation helps our readers more deeply understand themselves and the expectations—what you want to see—that they bring as they assume a certain genre for Genesis 1–11. As Calvin said, "Without knowledge of self there is no knowledge of God," and so it is with Scripture.[10] Unless we know what we want from the Bible, we cannot begin to understand its authors.

---

9. "A Curmudgeon's Guide to Praise." Posted October 12, 2013. *Los Angeles Review of Books.* *www.lareviewofbooks.org/essay/a-curmudgeons-guide-to-praise.* (Accessed July 21, 2014.)

10. John Calvin, *Institutes of the Christian Religion* (ed. John T. McNeill; trans. Ford Lewis Battles; 2 vols.; Philadelphia: Westminster, 1960), 1.35.

GENESIS 1 – 11 AS HISTORY AND THEOLOGY

JAMES K. HOFFMEIER

Introduction

Genesis 1–11 begins the story of redemption—the loss of God's presence; intimacy between God and humans,[1] and access to the tree of life. The narrative commences with "Paradise Lost" and culminates in the New Testament with "Paradise Regained," to borrow from one of John Milton's seventeenth-century classic poems. Because of the overarching theme connecting the early chapters of Genesis to the book of Revelation, Genesis 1–11 must be taken seriously. In recent centuries, especially because of the influence of Enlightenment rationalism on scriptural interpretation, readers of the Bible wonder whether Genesis can be read as it once was in pre-critical times. The dominant scientific worldview has understandably influenced the way Christians read the Bible in general and Genesis 1–11 in particular. A consequence of this hermeneutic has prompted the preoccupation of European biblical scholars to employ a "scientific" (*Wissenschaftlich*) approach that has sought to isolate the sources that stood behind Genesis, thereby denying the Jewish-Christian tradition of Mosaic authorship of the Pentateuch.

---

1. I heartily agree with Gordon Wenham's observations in his study, "Sanctuary Symbolism in the Garden of Eden Story," in *Proceedings of the Ninth World Congress of Jewish Studies, Division A: The Period of the Bible* (Jerusalem: World Union of Jewish Studies, 1986), 19–25 and reprinted in *I Studied Inscriptions from Before the Flood: Ancient Near Eastern, Literary, and Linguistic Approaches to Genesis 1–11* (eds. R. Hess & D. Tsumura: Winona Lake: Eisenbrauns, 1994), 399–404.

This short essay cannot devote time to the history of speculation about sources and origins of the book of Genesis, the so-called "critical" study of the Pentateuch. Consider, however, that the four-source hypothesis of Wellhausen that dominated biblical scholarship from the mid-nineteenth to the end of the twentieth century has been in "sharp decline," as E.W. Nicholson has observed and he admits, "some would say [it is] in a state of advanced rigor mortis."[2] Consequently, the "assured results" of critical scholarship are being rejected, ironically enough, by European Old Testament scholars![3]

The focus of the present work, rather, will be on the genre of the literature of Genesis 1–11 and the implications for interpretation of the texts that comprise it. I will also address the early Genesis narratives in a comparative manner with ancient Near Eastern literature in order to understand the relationship between the two.

Genesis: A Literary Overview

Genesis 1–11 is a convenient way of dividing the period from creation through the aftermath of the flood, sometimes called primeval history, from the Abrahamic narratives, plausibly set in the early second millennium BC. Some commentaries and studies are even divided accordingly.[4] This convenient packaging of Genesis 1–11, however, is an artificial division imposed on the text by modern interpreters, not one self-evident in the text of Genesis. David Clines has made this point in his thematic overview of Genesis, observing, "There is at no

2. E.W. Nicholson, *The Pentateuch in the Twentieth Century: The Legacy of Julius Wellhausen* (Oxford: Clarendon Press, 1998), 96.

3. See recent essays in Thomas Dozeman and Konrad Schmid (eds.), *A Farewell to the Yahwist? The Composition of the Pentateuch in Recent European Interpretation* (Atlanta: Society of Biblical Literature, 2006) and Thomas Dozeman, Thomas Römer, and Konrad Schmid (eds.), *Pentateuch, Hexateuch, or Enneateuch? Identifying Literary Words in Genesis through Kings* (Atlanta: Society of Biblical Literature, 2001).

4. Some examples of commentaries and studies on Genesis 1–11 include Robert Davidson, *Genesis 1–11* (Cambridge: Cambridge University Press, 1973); Patrick Miller, *Genesis 1–11: Studies in Structure and Theme* (Sheffield: JSOT Press, 1978); Louis Neveu, *Avant Abraham (Gen. 1–11)* (Angers: Université Catholique de l'Ouest, 1984); Isaac Kikiwada and Arthur Quinn, *Before Abraham Was: the Unity of Genesis 1–11* (Nashville: Abingdon, 1985); Claus Westermann, *Genesis 1–11: a Commentary* (Minneapolis: Fortress, 1994); John Rogerson, *Genesis 1–11: A Commentary* (Sheffield: JSOT, 1991); Ronald Hendel, *The Text of Genesis 1–11* (New York: Oxford University Press, 1998); Andrew Louth (ed.) *Genesis 1–11, Ancient Christian Commentary on Scripture* (Downers Grove: InterVarsity Press, 2001).

point a break between primaeval and patriarchal history."[5] Indeed, we are actually introduced to Abraham in Genesis 11:27–32, learning of his parentage, his original home in Chaldean Ur, his wife Sarah's barrenness, and about his migration with his father Terah and family to Canaan, which stalled in Haran.

This lack of a break between the primeval and patriarchal narratives is likely intentional. In his search for the "theme of the Pentateuch," Clines proposes that what unified these five books thematically is the promise to Abraham in Genesis 12:1–3, in which God pledges the patriarchal land, posterity, and a relationship (blessing) with him. The balance of Genesis and the four books that follow is on the fulfillment of the three facets of the promise, culminating in Joshua with the taking of the land.[6] When he turns to Genesis 1–11, Clines sees a pattern of "sin—speech (divine)—mitigation—punishment," making Genesis 1–11 "prefatory" to the promise,[7] that is, it necessarily explains the need for the promise.

One of the dangers of doing genre analysis of a large piece of ancient literature—be it in the Hebrew Bible, or Mesopotamian or Egyptian literature—is in imposing a single literary category on a work that is quite complex and made up of a variety of types of literature. Then too, one mistake of modern scholarship is to press onto ancient literature modern literary categories that did not exist in the ancient world. Even the system of dividing Genesis into fifty chapters is not original to the text but a later creation. The book of Genesis does in fact have its own organizational program, not one imposed by later scribes or interpreters. I maintain that working from the text, using clues within the book of Genesis itself, is the best way to read and understand the book as a whole and Genesis 1–11 as a vital unit of the larger work.

Genre of Genesis 1 - 11

Legend

One of the most influential figures in viewing Genesis as legend is Hermann Gunkel. At the end of the nineteenth and at the outset of

---

5. David J.A. Clines, *The Theme of the Pentateuch* (Sheffield: JSOT Press, 1978), 84.

6. Ibid., 9–65.

7. Ibid., 66–82.

the twentieth century, he argued that Genesis was comprised of sagas, or legendary stories that were transmitted orally over long periods of time before being recorded in written form.[8] "Inherent in the nature of legend," Gunkel maintained, is that "we cannot perceive ancient circumstances in them clearly, but only as though through a mist," and furthermore, that "legend poetically recast historical memories" by adding to them elements from other legends and characters.[9] Moreover, for Gunkel, Israel's legends are not solely the stories about the ancestors of Israel, but "they received them from abroad."[10] By this he meant that other ancient Near Eastern legends and myths made their way into Israel and into the Genesis narratives. Gunkel's category of "legend" primarily deals with Genesis 12–50, although he also describes the story of Noah as legend. However, the creation narratives he views quite differently, regarding them as myths, not unlike Babylonian creation myths that from his standpoint had only recently been discovered and translated.[11] Furthermore, he believed that the Babylonian "myth was brought over into Israel," where it lost "its mythological character" and was subsequently "Judaicized."[12]

In my judgment, the genre "legend" is inappropriate for Genesis as a whole. The inability to prove that certain characters existed, be they Adam, Noah, Nimrod, or Abram, does not make their stories legendary. We simply lack written materials to verify or reject elements of their stories.

Myth

Myth as a type of literature is widely accepted in biblical scholarship.[13] The problem with the literary category "myth" is that definitions abound, and there is a long tradition of regarding myth to be fiction,

---

8. Hermann Gunkel, *Schöpfung und Chaos in Urzeit un Endzeit* (Göttingen: Vandenhoeck, 1895), and further developed by Gunkel in *Genesis* (trans. Mark Biddle; Macon: Mercer University Press, 1997).

9. Gunkel, *Genesis*, xvi.

10. Ibid., xlviii.

11. Gunkel, *Schöpfung und Chaos* = translation in *Creation in the Old Testament* (ed. B.W. Anderson; Philadelphia: Fortress Press, 1984), 25–52.

12. Ibid, 49.

13. For example, see Bernard Batto, *Slaying the Dragon: Mythmaking in the Biblical Tradition* (Louisville: Westminster/John Knox Press, 1992) and *In the Beginning: Essays on the Creation Motifs in the Ancient Near East and the Bible* (Winona Lake: Eisenbrauns, 2013). I am grateful to Professor Batto who kindly gave me a copy of his new book.

opposite of history, something made up, even fantasy. Given this predisposition, it is understandable why conservative biblical scholars have been reluctant to use the term "myth."

The British Assyriologist, Andrew George, recently lamented that "there is little consensus as to what myth is and what it is not."[14] One definition of myth is "a timeless event in the world of the gods,"[15] which is appropriate for many ancient Near Eastern cosmologies. Kenton Sparks has identified four categories of myth, namely those pertaining to the psychological, metaphorical, historical, and pleasure.[16] Mircea Eliade, the great historian of religion, believed that "myth is bound up with ontology; it speaks only of *realities*, of what *really* happened, of what was fully manifested."[17] "Myth narrates a sacred history," Eliade maintained and it relates to "an event that took place in primordial Time, the fabled time of the 'beginnings.'"[18] The key idea here is that myth deals with what "*really* happened."

Thus myth, in the technical sense, is concerned with ultimate realities, not fiction. Even though preserved in the forms of stories or epic poems, myths are not fantasy. Peter Enns recently (and rightly) questioned "how much value there is in posing the choice of Genesis as either myth or history."[19] Myth is a type of literature that does not necessary look like historiography. It could be written in poetic form and may employ highly symbolic language, and yet, myth can be considered writing about real events. A classic example of this is the flood story, for which we not only have the biblical Hebrew report, but also a number of different Mesopotamian flood traditions (see further discussion of this below).

Lastly, to further illustrate that there may be no conflict between history and myth, it has been noted by historians that annalistic historical

---

14. Andrew George, *The Epic of Gilgamesh* (New York: Barnes & Noble, 1999), xxxiii.

15. Donald Redford, *Egypt, Canaan and Israel in Ancient Times* (Princeton: Princeton University Press, 1984), 409.

16. Kenton Sparks, "The Problem of Myth in Ancient Historiography," in *Rethinking the Foundations: Historiography in the Ancient World and in the Bible; Essays in Honour of John Van Seters* (eds. S.L. McKenzie & T. Römer; Berlin, de Gruyter, 2000), 271–77.

17. Mircea Eliade, *The Sacred & the Profane* (New York: Harcourt Brace Jovanovich, 1959), 95 (emphasis Eliade's).

18. Mircea Eliade, *Myth and Reality* (New York: Harper & Row, 1963), 5. Emphasis is Eliade's.

19. Peter Enns, *Inspiration and Incarnation* (Grand Rapids: Baker, 2005), 49.

records from the ancient biblical world used mythological images when speaking of historical events. The "Hero-god versus Chaos" motif, for example, is used in the reports of Ramesses II at the battle of Kadesh in the thirteenth century BC.[20] Sennacherib's annals, which include records of his campaign against Hezekiah's Judah in 701 BC, contain allusions to the cosmic struggle with Tiamat (the primeval sea), from the Babylonian creation myth *Enuma Elish*.[21]

Similarly, biblical authors used mythological motifs, even when writing about historical events and known individuals. Ezekiel, for instance, likens the reigning pharaoh (probably Hophra/Apries) to "a monster in the seas" (Ezek 32:2). Here, the biblical term *tannîn* references a sea monster known from Ugaritic literature. It is this same monster that the Old Testament states was mastered and defeated by God (see especially Isa 27:1, 51:9; Job 3:8, 41:1; Ps 74:14, 104:26). So Ezekiel saw no conflict in appropriating a mythological motif in service to a contemporary historical event.

Consequently, it is reasonable to assume that while Genesis 1–11 uses mythic language, that such language does not necessarily make its contents fiction. It may be, as I have argued elsewhere, that ancient Near Eastern creation motifs in Genesis 1 and 2 are primarily employed for polemical reasons against the prevailing worldviews of Mesopotamia, Canaan, and Egypt, all of which influenced ancient Israel.[22] Richard Averbeck has noticed other uses of ancient Near Eastern mythology in the creation chapters in Genesis, especially as "analogical thinking about history and reality."[23]

Family Histories

Before examining Genesis 1–11 as a unit, we need to step back and look at the entire book of Genesis. It has long been recognized that the

---

20. Redford, *Egypt, Canaan and Israel in Ancient Times*, 409.

21. K. Lawson Younger, "Assyrian Involvement in the Southern Levant at the End of the 8th Century B.C.E," in *Jerusalem in Bible and Archaeology: the First Temple Period* (eds. A. Vaughn & A.E. Killebrew; Atlanta: Society of Biblical Literature, 1993), 254–55.

22. James K. Hoffmeier, "Genesis 1 & 2 and Egyptian Cosmology," *Journal of the Ancient Near Eastern Society* 15 (1983), 39–49.

23. Richard Averbeck, "Ancient Near Eastern Mythography as It Relates to Historiography in the Hebrew Bible: Genesis 3 and the Cosmic Battle," in *The Future of Biblical Archaeology* (eds. J. Hoffmeier & A. Millard; Grand Rapids: Eerdmans, 2004), 328–56, esp. 355.

repeated phrase, "these are the generations" (KJV, RSV, ESV) or "this is the account" (NIV) is critical to understanding how the book is organized and, as will be suggested here, it is a key to identifying the genre of the book. The phrase employs the key Hebrew term *tôlēdôt* eleven times (Gen 2:4, 5:2, 6:9a, 10:1, 11:10a, 11:27a, 25:12, 25:19a, 36:1, 36:9, 37:2). As early as his commentary, first published in 1852, Franz Delitzsch recognized that this repeated refrain provides the organizational structure for the book of Genesis.[24] Later, in Delitzsch's classic commentary with C.F. Keil, the same analysis is offered,[25] thus dividing the book of Genesis by *tôlēdôt* formulae as follows:

History of the heavens and the earth (2:4b–4:26)
History of Adam (5:1–6:8)
History of Noah (6:9–9:26)
History of the sons of Noah (10:1–11:9)
History of Shem (11:10–26)
History of Terah (11:27–25:11)
History of Ishmael (25:12–18)
History of Isaac (25:19–35:29)
History of Esau (36:1–8 & 36:9–42)[26]
History of Jacob (37:1–50:26)

The *tôlēdôt* formula has limited use outside of Genesis, viz. Num 3:1; Ruth 4:18; 1 Chr 1:29. These references all deal with genealogies or family histories, making the usage of the *tôlēdôt* formulae consistent throughout the Old Testament. Yet in the book of Genesis, the formula is evidently deployed to organize smaller segments into a larger work, spanning the history of the world, beginning with creation and ending with Joseph's death in Egypt.[27]

---

24. Franz Delitzsch, *A New Commentary on Genesis* (revised edition, Edinburgh: T & T Clark, 1888), 60ff.

25. Franz Delitzsch and C.F. Keil, *Commentary on the Old Testament. Volume 1, The Pentateuch* (Edinburgh: T&T Clark, 1885), reprinted by Eerdmans, 5–6.

26. The formula occurs twice for Esau, Jacob's eldest son, in 36:1, 9. One can only speculate as to why this family history is divided into two parts.

27. For a recent treatment of the *tôlēdôt* as an organizing principle of the book, see Matthieu Richelle, "La structure littéraire de l'Histoire Primitive (Genèse 1,1–11,26) en son état final." *Biblische Notizen* 151 (2011): 3–22.

Likewise S.R. Driver, and many scholars since, recognized the importance of the *tôlēdôt* formula as providing a unified "plan" for Genesis, likely the work of the Priestly writer and compiler (of the sixth-fifth centuries BC) who utilized "pre-existing materials in the composition of his work."[28] Driver also thought the formula was used for genealogical purposes. Furthermore, Gerhard von Rad thought that the *tôlēdôt* formula was "the original framework for the Priestly narrative."[29] This early-twentieth-century understanding remains the view of scholars who still hold to the four-source hypothesis.[30]

Scholars who approach the Bible using more historical, exegetical methods and who appropriate newer literary approaches likewise recognize the centrality of the *tôlēdôt*.[31] Recently, Averbeck has written on the "genealogical framework" of Genesis, and considers that the *tôlēdôt* formula "shapes and unifies" the book.[32]

Genealogical texts in the ancient Near East, by their very nature, are treated seriously by scholars and not cavalierly dismissed as made up or fictitious, even if such lists are truncated or selective.[33] Donald Redford reminds us that genealogies in Egypt were "carefully kept."[34] Proof of this practice can be seen on a statue of the priest Basa, from the ninth century BC, who traces his priestly line back twenty-seven generations, to the early or mid-fifteenth century BC.[35] An even lon-

---

28. S.R. Driver, *The Book of Genesis* (London: Methuen & Co., 1909, 2nd ed.), ii–iv.

29. Gerhard von Rad, *Genesis, A Commentary*. Old Testament Library (Philadelphia: Westminster Press, 1972), 126.

30. E.S. Speiser, *Genesis*. The Anchor Bible (Garden City, NY: Doubleday, 1964), xxiv–xxvi. Coats, *Genesis with an Introduction to Narrative Literature* (Grand Rapids: Eerdmans, 1983) 19–21.

31. As a student of R.K. Harrison, I learned about the "tablet theory" behind the *tôlēdôt* that was advanced by P.J. Wiseman, *Creation Revealed in Six Days* (Edinburgh: Morgan and Scott, 1948), 34ff. His famous son, Donald Wiseman, the Assyriologist and Old Testament scholar, saw merit in aspects of his father's theory about the *tôlēdôt* in Genesis (see the forward to the reprinted version of P.J. Wiseman's earlier studies: *Clues to Creation in Genesis* [London: Marshall, Morgan & Scott, 1977], v–vii). See too R.K. Harrison, *Introduction to the Old Testament* (Grand Rapids: Eerdmans, 1969), 548–51.

32. Averbeck, "Ancient Near Eastern Mythography as It Relates to Historiography in the Hebrew Bible: Genesis 3 and the Cosmic Battle," 343.

33. See my discussion on king-lists in *COS* 1:68.

34. Donald Redford, *Pharaonic King-list, Annals and Day-books* (Missisauga: Benben, 1986), 62, n. 226.

35. Robert Ritner, "Denderite Temple Hierarchy and the Family of Nefwenenef," in *For His Ka: Essays Offered in Memory of Klaus Baer* (ed. D. Silverman; Chicago: The Oriental Institute), 205–26.

ger genealogical span is preserved on the Assyrian King List,[36] dating from the reign of Shalmaneser V (726–722 BC) to around 2000 BC, to the earliest Assyrian rulers "who lived in tents."[37] Private genealogies and king lists were recorded and, as far as we can tell, were an accurate accounting of family histories and dynasties. Priestly genealogies were important to confer priestly offices on individuals, but royal lists had an important civil function. Alan Millard observes such lists had to be accurate because, "legal deeds had to be concluded" based on them and "they enabled kings to learn when their predecessors had built temples or palaces which they were rebuilding."[38]

It has been rightly noted by Richard Hess that the genealogies of Genesis do not find an exact parallel with ancient Near Eastern counterparts.[39] The differences in form, he suggests, are due to the differences in function. He is undoubtedly correct, but the differences in function do not mean that both the Genesis genealogies and those from the ancient Near East were not interested in an accurate and orderly sequence of ancestors. Lists could be truncated and schematically organized, but the names refer to real people, not fictitious figures. And this is the essential point for our discussion here.

The point of this excursus is to show that genealogical lists (with which Genesis abounds) and history (especially family histories) are closely related. This brings us back to the word *tôlĕdôt*. Recognizing the historical nature of genealogies, some scholars render this key word as "record"[40] or "history."[41] I think Gordon Wenham captures the essence of *tôlĕdôt* by rendering it "this is the family history of X."[42]

---

36. Of course, with king lists, there are different dynasties in play, although there may be a biological link between families. The numbering of dynasties used by historians of Egypt follows the system set in place by Manetho (the Ptolemaic period priest-historian), which seems to have been rooted in earlier traditions like that in the Turin King List. In some instances, there could be biological connections between royal families, like Dynasty 4 and 5, and certainly between 17 and 18.

37. Alan Millard, "Assyrian King Lists," *COS* 1:463–65.

38. Ibid., 461.

39. Richard Hess, "The Genealogies of Genesis 1–11 and Comparative Literature," *Biblica* 70 (1989), 241–54.

40. Speiser, *Genesis*, 39.

41. KBL 1700; Umberto Cassuto, *A Commentary of the Book of Genesis* (2 vols.; trans. Israel Abrahams; Jerusalem: Magnes Press, 1961), 1:273; Gordon Wenham, *Genesis 1–15*, Word Biblical Commentary (Waco: Word, 1987), 4, 16.

42. Wenham, *Genesis 1–15*, 119, 149, 209, etc.

By using the formula "this is the family history," the author or compiler signals the genre of the book of Genesis, including chapters 1–11. Even if we concede that earlier records were used, the "family history" structuring of the book indicates that the narratives should be understood as historical, focusing on the origins of Israel back to Adam and Eve, the first human couple and parents of all humanity. The use of a genealogical-historical framework for Genesis points the reader towards how the book as a whole should be understood, namely, the narratives are dealing with real events involving historical figures — and this includes Genesis 1–11.

Having addressed the broader question of genre, let us turn now to some specific passages to examine the probing question of how they represent real events, that is, how they reflect events or memories of events that actually occurred centuries and even millennia before being put into writing.

Case Studies
The Garden of Eden

In order to lay the foundation for the narratives about the Nephilim, the flood, and the Tower of Babel, which will receive major treatment below, let us first go back to the garden of Eden narrative to provide a basis for my approach to the later episodes. If any passage in the Bible has been called "myth" it is Genesis 2:8–3:24; it contains reports of creating Eve out of Adam's rib, there are mystical trees, a talking snake, direct communication between God and humans, and angelic guardians (cherubim) posted at the entrance of Eden.

These considerations notwithstanding, the author of the narrative goes to great lengths to place Eden within the known geography of the ancient Near East, not some made-up mythological, Narnia-like wonderland. Indeed, Gerhard von Rad noted that with Genesis 2:10–14, "we find ourselves in our historical and geographical world,"[43] and E.A. Speiser concurred, declaring that Eden's "physical setting cannot be dismissed offhand as sheer imagination."[44] From the following description

---

43. von Rad, *Genesis*, 79.

44. E.A. Speiser, "The Rivers of Paradise," in *Festschrift Johannes Friedrich zum 65. Geburtsag am 27. August 1958 gewidment* (ed. A. Moortgat et al.; Heidelberg: Carl Winter, 1959), 473.

an ancient hearer or reader of Genesis 2:10–14 would have immediately recognized that Eden was specifically located somewhere in Mesopotamia:

> A river watering the garden flowed from Eden; from there it was separated into four headwaters. The name of the first is the Pishon; it winds through the entire land of Havilah, where there is gold. (The gold of that land is good; aromatic resin and onyx are also there.) The name of the second river is the Gihon; it winds through the entire land of Cush. The name of the third river is the Tigris; it runs along the east side of Asshur. And the fourth river is the Euphrates.

Evidently, the garden was located at the confluence of four rivers, and they are named. In the case of the first three, additional geographical information is offered to help pinpoint their courses. The third and fourth rivers are immediately recognizable. The Hebrew term for Euphrates (based on the Greek rendering), *pĕrāt*, comes from the Akkadian term *purattu*, the ancient name of the river.[45] Noteworthy is the fact that no description of location is offered because none was necessary. The third river is the Tigris, another river whose name and location remain identifiable. The Hebrew term, *ḥideqel*, derives from the Sumerian name of the river, *Idigna/gin*, which entered Akkadian as *(I)dig/lat*.[46] Genesis offers only that this river "flows east of Asshur." Asshur, or Assyria, in ancient times occupied the northern part of Mesopotamia, present-day Iraq.

The identity of the other two rivers remains uncertain, and no doubt their obscurity is why geographical data about their locations is much greater and detailed. The name Havilah is used in the OT to refer to Arabia, a location known for its frankincense[47] and where fine gold was mined up through the nineteenth century.[48]

The name Pishon means "to jump or skip,"[49] apparently a descriptive name not unlike the Gihon. A possible candidate for the now

---

45. KBL 2:978–79.
46. KBL 1:293.
47. W.W. Müller, "Frankincense," *ABD* II, 854.
48. W.W. Müller, "Havilah," in *ABD* III, 82.
49. W.W. Müller, "Pishon," in *ABD* V, 374.

defunct Pishon River was discovered with the aid of Shuttle Imaging Radar technology. It evidently flowed east from the mountainous Hijaz region of Saudi Arabia. Dr. Farouk el-Baz, the geologist and director of the Center for Remote Sensing at Boston University, discovered traces of its course beneath the sand with ground penetrating radar images from the Space Shuttle.[50] Because the river flowed east towards Kuwait (where the Tigris and Euphrates debouche into the Persian Gulf) el-Baz named it the "Kuwait River." James Sauer immediately saw the geographical connection between this ancient river and the description of the Pishon in Genesis 2.[51] The "Kuwait River" appears to have dried up sometime late in the third millennium BC. The fact Genesis 2 knows about this river is remarkable indeed.

The fourth river, the Gihon, which "winds through the entire land of Cush," remains unidentified. Cush, or Kush, refers to more than one geographical area in the Bible, the most prominent being Nubia, the southern part of Egypt and Sudan (2 Kgs 19:9; Isa 18:1; 20:3; Ezek 29:10; Esth 1:1). The other location, which better fits the Mesopotamian setting of the other rivers and of Eden, is Babylonia (central Iraq) itself. This squares with the name "Kassites," from the word *kuššu*, an obscure people who gained control of Babylonia after the fall of Hammurabi's dynasty around 1600 BC.[52] The "Kassite dynasty" based in Babylon spans from the fifteenth through twelfth centuries BC, and it is during this period that central Mesopotamia would be known as Cush (Kush) in the ancient Near East, and to the biblical writer.

"Gihon" means "bubbling water," "gush forth,"[53] and hence is descriptive of this (fast flowing?) river. Gihon is also the name of the bubbling spring of Jerusalem (cf. 1 Kgs 1:33, 38, 45; 2 Chr 32:30).

The point of the foregoing is to demonstrate that Genesis seeks to place the garden of Eden in historical ancient Mesopotamia and so offers minutiae (the ancient equivalent of coordinates) so that the reader could locate it. This does not look like "a timeless event set in the world

50. Farouk El-Baz, "A River in the Desert," *Discover*, July 1993.

51. James A. Sauer, "The River Runs Dry," *Biblical Archaeology Review* 22, No. 4 (1996): 52–54, 57, 64.

52. Diana Stein, "Kassites," in *OEANE* 3, 271–75. Speiser, "The Rivers of Paradise," 475.

53. KBL 189.

of the gods."[54] Consequently, though the garden pericope may contain mythic elements, it is set in "our historical and geographical world,"[55] which is hard to reconcile with pure mythology.

The Sons of God and the Daughters of Man (Gen 6:1 - 4)

The literary context of this narrative must be established before delving into a discussion of genre and interpretation. It has been common to view this episode as having no connection to the preceding genealogical chapter (Gen 5), where the former is considered to be from the Priestly (P) source and Genesis 6:1–8 a continuity of the Yahwists (J) narrative that stopped in 4:26.[56]

In recent years, exciting developments have been made in the literary study of Genesis, an approach that treats the book as literature, as opposed to the atomistic approach of source criticism that seeks to chop the text up into artificial units. This new movement began in the late 1960s, with James Muilenburg's seminal essay "Form Criticism and Beyond,"[57] that stimulated many important studies by scholars like Leland Ryken,[58] Kenneth Gros Louis,[59] Robert Alter[60] and others. Literary or rhetorical approaches seek to examine the broad tapestry of the text rather than simply isolating threads.

In response to classical source critical approaches to Genesis 1–11 that see the chapters as a patchwork of sources sometimes clumsily put together, Jack Sasson countered that "it might be well worth our while to seek a solution which does not depend so heavily on documentary separation, but one which would retain a healthy respect for the literary sensitivity of redactors."[61] He identified six literary units in Genesis

---

54. Redford, *Egypt, Canaan and Israel in Ancient Times*, 409.

55. von Rad, *Genesis*, 79.

56. Driver, *The Book of Genesis*, 82; von Rad, *Genesis*, 113; George Coats, *Genesis with an Introduction to Narrative Literature*, 84–86.

57. Published in *JBL* 88 (1969): 1–18.

58. I had the privilege of taking Leland Ryken's course, "the Bible as Literature" (Spring 1973), the first time he taught the course. His book appeared soon thereafter: *The Literature of the Bible* (Grand Rapids: Zondervan, 1974).

59. Kenneth Gros Louis, *Literary Interpretations of Biblical Narratives* (Nashville: Abingdon Press, 1974).

60. Robert Alter, *The Art of Biblical Narrative* (New York: Basic Books, 1981).

61. Jack Sasson, "The 'Tower of Babel' as a Clue to the Redactional Structuring of the Primeval Structuring of the Primeval History (Genesis 1:1–11:9)," in *The Bible World: Essays in Honor of Cyrus H. Gordon* (ed. G. Rendsburg, et al.; New York: KTAV, 1980), 211.

1:1–6:8 that are paralleled by the same thematic pattern that follows in Genesis 6:9–11:9. He further noticed that the parallel units are balanced by ten generations from creation to Noah and ten from the flood to Abram:[62]

Creation(s) (Gen 1:1-2:14)	The Flood and its Aftermath (Gen 6:9-9:2)
Warning and Covenant with Man (2:15-24)	Warning and Covenant with Man (9:3-17)
The Fall (3)	[no equivalent]
Cain and Abel (4:1-16)	Curse of Canaan (9:18-27)
Mankind's Ancestries (4:17-5:32)	Nations of the Earth (10)
The Nephilim (6:1-8)	Tower of Babel (11:1-9)

According to this literary analysis, the Nephilim episode stands opposite the Tower of Babel. In both narratives, we find human arrogance resulting in judgment. Sasson's understanding of Genesis 1–11 places Genesis 6:1–8 in the genealogy of the first ten generations, and I might add, it is also included in the second *tōlĕdôt* unit, while the third begins with 6:9.

Gary Rendsburg has warmly embraced Sasson's conclusions and advanced them further by showing that key words and phrases are found within the parallel sections.[63] Thematically, the two episodes run in opposite directions. In Genesis 6, Rendsburg observes, we learn that "the gods came down to the human realm; and the Tower of Babel story tells of man's efforts to reach the divine realm."[64] In both stories, the "name" or reputation of the characters is involved; in Genesis 6:1–4 the Nephilim are "the men of renown" (lit. "men of the name," *ʾanšê hāšēm*), whereas in the Tower of Babel story, the motivation for building the tower is: "let us make a name for ourselves."

On the literary level, then, these two stories occupy the same place structurally in the narrative sequence (i.e. at the end of the long literary block), with the Nephilim story representing the culmination of

---

62. Sasson, "The 'Tower of Babel' as a Clue to the Redactional Structuring of the Primeval Structuring of the Primeval History (Genesis 1:1–11:9)," 214–19. A Similar analysis was independently reached by Bernhard Anderson a few years before Sasson's publication, "From Analysis to Synthesis: The Interpretation of Genesis 1–11," *JBL* 97 (1978): 23–39.

63. Gary Rendsburg, *The Redaction of Genesis* (Winona Lake: Eisenbrauns, 1986), 7–26, especially 20–21.

64. Ibid., 21.

humanity's rebellion against God that began in the garden. The stories leading up to the rebellion, Cain's murder of Abel (Gen 4:8) followed by Lamech's slaying of a young man (4:23–24), prompted the LORD's resolve (6:5–8) to destroy humanity. Thus Genesis 6:1–8 serves as a link to the flood story and the second literary block (6:9–11:9).[65] Additionally, the *tōlēdôt* of Noah marks the beginning of this new unit (6:9). While the consequences of the actions of the tower builders lead to the dispersion of humanity, the "evil" of the sons of god and the daughters of man results in the flood. In contrast to the evil on the earth that seems to be spinning out of control (6:5–6), Noah's life was exemplary; God considered him to be "a righteous man, blameless in his generation" and "Noah walked with God" (6:9). God then worked through Noah to restore humanity. Likewise, in the aftermath of the dispersion of humanity after the Babel incident (11:1–9), we are introduced to a new individual through whom God would bless humanity, namely, Abram (11:26–32). And with both Noah and Abram, the LORD makes a covenant.

Having considered the structure of Genesis 1–11 and some of the literary and linguistic connections between the "sons of God and daughters of man" and Tower of Babel episodes, let us turn to focus directly on Genesis 6:1–4, which has rightly been called "one of the obscurest in the Pentateuch,"[66] and yet it occupies a significant place as a precursor to the flood narrative. Scholars such as Gunkel,[67] Speiser,[68] Brueggemann,[69] and Coats,[70] whose works span nearly a century, have identified this story as myth.

The heart of the problem is identifying the "sons of God" (*běnê ha'ĕlōhîm*). If they are divine beings or angels, as traditionally interpreted, then we appear to have a classical mythological motif, viz. gods and humans intermingling and reproducing demi-gods, super humans.

---

65. The idea that Genesis 6:1–4 has a dual function of concluding the preceding section and introducing the following is accepted by some commentators, e.g. Victor Hamilton, *The Book of Genesis Chapters 1–17* (Grand Rapids: Eerdmans, 1990), 261.

66. Cassuto, *A Commentary of the Book of Genesis*, 1:291.

67. Gunkel, *Genesis*, 56–57.

68. Speiser, *Genesis*, 45.

69. Walter Brueggemann, *Genesis, A Commentary for Teaching and Preaching* (Atlanta: John Knox Press, 1982), 70–71.

70. Coats, *Genesis with an Introduction to Narrative Literature*, 84–86.

The Hebrew word *nĕpilîm* derives from the root *npl*, which means "fall."[71] This meaning supports the view of some that these are fallen ones, i.e. fallen angels (see below). The grammatical form of *nĕpilîm*, however, is not passive and so cannot be translated "fallen ones." In Genesis 6:4, the Nephilim are described as the offspring of the sons of God (or gods) and the daughters of man. The Septuagint renders the Hebrew *hannĕpilîm* as "giants," undoubtedly because Hellenistic, Jewish scribes interpreted the term in light of Numbers 13:33. This rendering clearly has nothing to do with the meaning "fall."

The reference to the Nephilim (*hannĕpilîm*) being in the land of Canaan by Moses' spies in Numbers 13 seems odd, since one would assume they were eliminated in the flood. Nahum Sarna makes a sensible suggestion that the use of *hannĕpilîm* here is "for oratorical effect, much as 'Huns' was used to designate Germans during two world wars."[72] In other words, the Israelite spies saw Nephilim-like men in Canaan.

What can be said of the *nĕpilîm* is that they were "mighty men who were of old, the men of renown" (ESV) or "they were the heroes of old, men of renown" (NIV). "Mighty men" (*gibbōrîm*) has to do with a military champion: David was so labeled (1 Sam 16:18), so was Goliath (1 Sam 17:51), and Jephthah the warrior judge (Judges 1:11). Genesis 6:4 describes these mighty men or heroes as *mēʿôlām*, literally "from of old" or ancient times. The term seems to be a general chronological marker from the standpoint of the author.

In the Sumerian Epic of Gilgamesh, we learn about a legendary figure described as being of "heroic stature" ... "tall, magnificent and terrible" ... "two-thirds of him god and one third human."[73] Extant colossal statues of Gilgamesh from Neo-Assyrian sites (first millennium BC) depict the hero holding a lion in his arm, as one might hold a cat. The portrayal of this larger than life figure, deemed part-divine, is of a legendary king whose name appears as the fifth king of the first Dynasty of Uruk on the Sumerian King List. This suggests that he was

71. KBL 1:709.
72. Nahun Sarna, *Genesis: The JPS Torah Commentary* (Philadelphia: Jewish Publication Society, 1989), 46.
73. George, *The Epic of Gilgamesh*, 2.

a real king, a historical figure who was king in Sumer around 2750 BC.[74] Thus, unlike the folkloristic figure of Paul Bunyan, whose tales appear not to be based on an actual man, the legendary tales about Gilgamesh rest on a historical character.

Not all interpreters accept that the "sons of God/gods" were angels. The twelfth century Jewish sage Ibn Ezra, for example, thought that judges or sons of princes were intended.[75] The great medieval savant Rashi translated the enigmatic expression "sons of nobles."[76] More recently, Umberto Cassuto argued that there were different categories of angels, but the messengers of God, commonly known as mal'ākîm elsewhere in Genesis, are always noble and honorable servants of God.[77] Hence "sons of God/gods" in Genesis 6 cannot be confused with divine angels. Rather, Cassuto contended that they are evil spirits (cf. 1 Sam 16:14; 1Kgs 22:22) from the divine council.[78] After all, in Job 1:6, Satan was among the běnê hā'ĕlōhîm.

Early Christian interpreters also wrestled with this passage. They were undoubtedly influenced by their reading of the Septuagint, which rendered běnê hā'ĕlōhîm as "angels of God." The tendency among early Christian commentators was to understand the běnê hā'ĕlōhîm as "fallen" angels. This was the interpretation of Clement of Alexandria (ca. AD 150–215) and others.[79] Calvin dismissed such an interpretation. For him the idea of divine beings (regardless of type) being able to reproduce with humans was absurd.[80] He preferred to see "sons of God" as those who had been divinely adopted as sons and hence in a relationship with God, though they eventually departed from God and lusted after woman. The problem with his interpretation is that it does not sufficiently explain how spiritually rebellious men sired the mighty Nephilim!

74. Ibid., xxxi.

75. Abraham ben Meir Ibn Ezra, *Commentary on the Pentateuch: Bereshit* (trans. H.N. Strickman & A.M. Silver; New York: Menorah Publishing 1988), 93.

76. Online version from www.chabad.org.

77. Cassuto, *A Commentary of the Book of Genesis* 1:290–94.

78. Ibid., 294.

79. Louth (ed.), *Genesis 1–11*, 123–24.

80. John Calvin, *Commentary on Genesis* (Christian Classic Ethereal Library: www.ccel. org).

Along the lines of Calvin's interpretation, some early Christian church leaders thought this Genesis story was about the marriage between the godly line of Seth and the ungodly line of Cain. Such was the view of Ephrem, the Syrian from the fourth century, whose interpretation was followed by none other than Augustine.[81] These differing views of the early Christian and Jewish commentators are still, remarkably, embraced by modern interpreters.[82]

More recent interpreters have wrestled with what looks like myth in Genesis 6. Sarna acknowledges that while "at first glance" the story of the divine beings reproducing with human women looks like ancient mythology, it is more likely that Genesis 6 preserves a "highly condensed version of the original story" whose function was "to combat polytheistic mythology."[83] He concludes:[84]

> The picture presented here of celestial beings intermarrying with women of earth may partake of the mythical, but it does not overstep the bounds of monotheism; there is only one God who passes judgment and makes decisions. The offspring of such unnatural union may have possessed heroic stature, but they have no divine qualities; they are flesh and blood like all humans.

Cassuto was well aware of the influences of ancient Near Eastern "concepts" and myths and therefore maintained that the Torah was "in conflict with certain ideas that had already found their way into the ranks of our people."[85] Wenham suggests that the Nephilim pericope "comes closer to myth than anywhere else" in the OT, but because the old story is so brief (with Sarna), it had "been effectively demythologized."[86] There is something to this idea. The Torah displays an aversion for myth, and as suggested above, combating the ancient Near Eastern mythologies is overtly and subtly at work in the book of Genesis. An example of this antipathy can be seen in Genesis 1:16

---

81. Louth (ed.), Genesis 1–11, 123–24.

82. E.g. Delitzsch, A New Commentary on Genesis, 222. Hamilton, The Book of Genesis Chapters 1–17, 265 considers this theory a possibility.

83. Nahum Sarna, Genesis: The JPS Torah Commentary (Philadelphia: Jewish Publication Society, 1989), 45.

84. Ibid.

85. Cassuto, A Commentary of the Book of Genesis 1:7.

86. Wenham, Genesis 1–15, 138.

where sun and moon are labeled "greater light" and "lesser light," instead of the expected words, probably because the Hebrew terms *šemeš* and *yārēaḥ* were also treated as the names for the sun and moon deities in the Semitic world. Claus Westermann believes that Genesis 2:15, when treating God's command for Adam to "work and keep" the garden, "strips work of any mythical connection with the world of the gods."[87]

Because of this tendency to be anti-myth (that is, accepting the polytheistic assumptions of ancient Near Eastern mythology), could it be that in Genesis 6 we have an ancient (as the term *mēʿôlām*— "of old" suggests) and authentic story, that in the course of time had been mythologized and part of the shared memory of the ancient Near East, but was demythologized for the Israelite audience when recorded? In the end, I contend that despite our inability to completely understand this short episode, it must recall a genuine memory from early human history; after all, it is held up as the "final straw" that caused God to determine to judge creation— "The LORD saw that the wickedness of man was great on the earth, and that every intent of the thoughts of his heart was only evil continually" ... "I will blot out man whom I have created ..." (Gen 6:5, 7 NASB). God the judge determined that the verdict to destroy much of his creation was in order, and that he would start over with Noah and his wife (and family), a second Adam and Eve.[88] For God to resolve to wipe out humans on the earth would surely not be the result of some made up story!

Flood Stories and Traditions

Mesopotamian Traditions

In 2014, this well-known biblical story was made into a feature length movie, simply called "Noah," starring Russell Crowe and directed by Darren Aronofsky. Naturally, this movie prompted public interest in the question of the historicity of the Genesis story. What makes the study of the flood narrative in Genesis so intriguing is that since the late nineteenth century, OT scholars have had to take into account

---

87. Westermann, *Genesis 1–11*, 222.
88. On the literary connections between Adam and Eve and Noah and his wife, see Rendsburg, *The Redaction of Genesis*, 9–13.

the Mesopotamian flood traditions which share much in common with Noah's story.

The discovery of the first ancient flood story was made in Nineveh in 1872, found in the famous library of Ashurbanipal (668–631 BC). The flood story is found within the Gilgamesh Epic, undoubtedly the most celebrated piece of literature from ancient Mesopotamia. It has survived in more than 70 textual witnesses, some copies of which were found in the old Hittite capital of Ḥattuša (central Turkey), and was even translated into Hittite and Hurrian (the language of the Mittani Kingdom in north Syria). Akkadian copies were also discovered on tablets at Emar (present-day Syria), Ugarit, and in Canaan at Megiddo, all dating to the fourteenth century BC.[89] So it is patently clear that this version of the flood epic was known and studied as a part of the scribal curriculum during the second millennium BC when Babylonian or Akkadian served as the language of international communication.

Even Egypt, with its long and proud tradition of producing texts and literature in hieroglyphics and hieratic (a shorthand of hieroglyphics), when corresponding to ancient Near Eastern kings, wrote on cuneiform tablets, as is evident by the discovery of nearly four-hundred tablets and fragments at Tell el-Amarna, pharaoh Akhenaten's capital in middle Egypt (ca. 1347–1336 BC).[90] Most of these documents were diplomatic communiqués from the ancient Near East to Egypt; however, the Amarna archive also produced literary texts, including the Adapa Myth and Nergal and Erishkigal. It is inconceivable that the Gilgamesh Epic was unknown in Egypt, especially since lesser known literary works were documented. Thus, Akkadian literature would have been studied by Egyptian scribes who dealt with international communications.

In light of Mesopotamian literary texts discovered in Egypt (and surely there were many more that either have not survived or await discovery in other archives), and the Gilgamesh Epic (or parts thereof) attested at Megiddo (which was under Egyptian control during the Late Bronze Age, ca. 1450–1200 BC), it is noteworthy that we currently lack an Egyptian flood story. The absence suggests that knowledge of, and

---

89. George, *The Epic of Gilgamesh*, xxvi–xxvii and 132–140.

90. For a general study and translation of the Amarna cache, see William Moran, *The Amarna Letters* (Baltimore: Johns Hopkins University, 1992).

access to, a Mesopotamian story, myth, or legend does not necessarily mean that the recipient culture borrowed, adapted, or transformed the particular literary tradition! This is a cautionary note for those who insist that literary borrowing was the normal practice between ancient Near Eastern cultures, especially between Israel and her neighbors (particularly Canaanite and Mesopotamian).

The closest tradition in Egypt to the divinely initiated destruction of humans is the so-called "Destruction of Mankind," known in Egyptian as "The Book of the Cow of Heaven."[91] The plot of this text is that the aging Sun-god Re experienced a rebellious plot by humans. In response, Re wanted vengeance, and so he summoned the leonine goddess Sakhmet to slaughter humanity. After relentless attacks, Re repents and does not want everyone destroyed. While it took some subterfuge to pacify Sakhmet's out-of-control rage, humans were spared annihilation. In this Egyptian tale, copies of which are found only in royal tombs from ca. 1327–1136 BC,[92] there is no account of a flood, no righteous human hero, no ark, and no thankful worship after the catastrophe.

While there is no flood or "ark" tradition in Egypt per se, the Hebrew flood story may have picked up a very critical Egyptian word that is used in Genesis 6–9, and that is the word for "ark" itself. The Hebrew term *tēbāh* is used twenty-three times in the Noah account, and is thought by some scholars to be a loanword from the Egyptian root *tbt*, a word for a chest,[93] box, or sarcophagus (i.e. a rectangular-shaped wooden box). Interestingly the only other time *tēbāh* occurs in the OT is in the Moses story (set in Egypt), where his reed ark (*tēbāh*) is placed in the Nile waters (Exod 2:3, 5). A symbolic connection between

---

91. Miriam Lichtheim, "The Destruction of Mankind," *COS* 1:36.

92. Ibid., 36.

93. KBL 2:1678. Cassuto, *A Commentary of the Book of Genesis*, 59. For a lengthy treatment of *tēbāh* see James K. Hoffmeier, *Israel in Egypt* (New York: Oxford University Press, 1997), 138. Regarding *tēbāh* in Exodus, see Cornelius Houtman, *Exodus: Historical Commentary on the Old Testament* 1 (Kampen: Kok, 1993), 275. Chayim Cohen has questioned the connection of *tēbāh* to the Egyptian term in that the latter never means boat (see "Hebrew *tbh*: Proposed Etymologies," *JANES* 4 (1972) : 37–51), however, I would argue that *tēbāh* in Genesis does not refer to just any simple boat, otherwise words like *ṣi* or *'ŏniyāh* could have been used. The use of *tēbāh*, rather, seems to be used for its symbolic connection to the Moses story.

the two narratives is evident; in both, a hero is used to bring salvation to people.[94]

In a book that was released just as the present study was underway,[95] the British Museum Assyriologist, Irving Finkel has proposed an Akkadian etymology to explain the origins of the word *tēbāh* in Genesis. He posits that the Babylonian word *tubbû* stands behind *tēbāh*. This Babylonian word occurs just twice in a single tablet that dates to around 500 BC and its meaning is obscure, although it is certainly associated with boating; the Akkadian word *eleppu* (the word for "ark" in Atrahasis) is used alongside *tubbû* in this text.[96] At first glance, the words look like a match, but the Babylonian word starts with the letter *tet* whereas the Hebrew begins with the consonant *taw*; so the two do not correspond linguistically to one another. Finkel acknowledges this linguistic problem, but nevertheless forges ahead with his theory, believing that the Babylonian word was "Hebraized."[97] Assyriologist Alan Millard, who (along with W.G. Lambert) published the Epic of Atrahasis, has correctly critiqued Finkel for trying "to explain the obscure Hebrew word by a more obscure Babylonian one!"[98]

For the present, we shall have to remain uncertain about the origin of the Hebrew word *tēbāh*. Although, I am inclined to agree with the Egyptian etymology until a more convincing one replaces it.

Having examined the extent to which the Gilgamesh flood story is found outside of Mesopotamia, and the role of Mesopotamian literature in Egypt, let us return to investigate other Mesopotamian flood traditions. There is a Sumerian version of the flood story, in which the flood hero is name Ziusudra.[99] This text is from the mid-second millennium BC, but surely originated in earlier times when the Sumerian language was dominant in Mesopotamia (ca. pre–2000 BC). Though quite fragmentary, it records that the gods had resolved to flood the earth, but their reason is lost. Ziusudra is introduced as a pious king who is warned

---

94. Sarna, *Genesis*, 52.

95. Irving Finkel, *The Ark Before Noah* (New York/London: Doubleday, 2014), 147–48.

96. W.G. Lambert and A.R. Millard, *Atra-Ḥasis: The Babylonian Story of the Flood* (Oxford: Oxford University Press, 1969), 178.

97. Finkel, *The Ark Before Noah*, 149.

98. A.R. Millard, review of *The Ark Before Noah* in *Evangelicals Now* (April 2014), 14.

99. M. Civil, "The Sumerian Flood Story," in Lambert and Millard, *Atra-Ḥasis*," 138–45.

of the coming deluge (ll. 140–160).[100] Reference to building a boat is lost, but the text resumes with the storm lasting seven days and nights (ll. 201–205); the sun comes out and "Ziusudra made an opening in the huge boat" (ll. 206); the righteous hero then worships the Sun-god and is granted eternal life like a god.

The points in common with the Genesis flood narrative are even more striking in the Gilgamesh Epic. Here the hero goes on a journey to seek the secret to eternal life, after the death of his friend and partner in adventure, Enkidu.[101] His travels took him to visit Utnapishtim, the Noah figure,[102] to learn how he obtained eternal life. Utnapishtim then recounts the flood story. Here we learn of the decisions of the divine council, headed by the sky god Anu, to send a flood (no reason given), but that the god Ea broke ranks with the gods and divulged the plan to Utnapishtim through the wall of his hut (apparently in a dream):[103] "Man of Shuruppak, son of Ubartutu, destroy this house, build a ship, forsake possessions, seek life, build an ark and save life."[104] Ea then goes on to give instructions on building the ark that would be seven decks high with an overall shape of a cube. It was then to be caulked in order to make it waterproof. Upon completion, Utnapishtim took his family and relatives on board, along with craftsmen and animals, before the ferocious storm broke. So overwhelming was the downpour that the gods panicked! "The gods cowered like dogs, crouching outside, Ishtar screamed like a woman in childbirth."[105] After seven days and nights of storm, Utnapishtim's ark landed on Mount Nimush, or Nisir (in the land of Gutium, thought to be in the Zagros mountains east of the Tigris).[106] Like Noah in the Genesis account (8:6–12), Utnapishtim released a dove to see if the waters had sufficiently abated. Then a swallow was sent out, and lastly a raven. As in the biblical story, the first two return, but the third does not, indicating the land was ready for humans and animals once again. After disembarking, Utnapishtim made offerings,

---

100. These are the line numbers used by Civil.

101. George, *The Epic of Gilgamesh*, 1–131.

102. For another translation of just the flood portion of the Gilgamesh Epic, see Benjamin Foster, "Gilgamesh," in *COS* 1:458–60.

103. Ibid., 460.

104. Ibid., 458.

105. Ibid., 459.

106. Ibid., 460, n. 5.

and the gods (who had been deprived of food for two weeks!) "smelled the sweet savor" and they "crowded around the sacrificer like flies."[107]

This flood epic is written in poetic form and is consistently labeled "myth" by Assyriologists. It is worth noting, however, that Utnapishtim is identified as being from the Sumerian city of Shurupak and the son of Ubartutu, the last king of Shuruppak before the deluge, according to the Sumerian King List.[108] Shuruppak has been identified with the site of Fara, south of Baghdad, whose earliest remains go back to the late fourth millennium BC.[109] Then too, Gilgamesh, as noted previously, is believed to have been the historic king of Uruk around 2750 BC. The foregoing suggests, even though the Gilgamesh Epic (with its flood story) has mythic elements and deals with legendary heroes, its events are set in the Tigris-Euphrates Valley (and just outside of it to the northeast where the ark ends up).

The next Mesopotamian flood tradition to consider here is the Babylonian Epic of Atrahasis. A.R. Millard and W.G. Lambert, who published the most complete Akkadian version of the Atrahasis Epic, maintain that it is the source from which the Gilgamesh Epic obtained its flood story.[110] The details about the flood, boat, animals, etc. in the two versions are virtually identical. What Atrahasis uniquely provides is the pre-history of the flood.[111] It begins with the creation of humans as a response to the desires of the gods to pass off to someone else the drudgery of their work, like canal digging. The gods made their demands known to the superior deities:[112]

> Let the birth-goddess create offspring (?)
> And let man bear the toil of the gods...
> Let him bear the yoke assigned by Enlil,
> Let man carry the toil of the gods...
> Let him give me the clay so that I can make it

---

107. Ibid., 460.

108. Samuel Noah Kramer, *The Sumerians* (Chicago: University of Chicago, 1963), 328.

109. Harriet Martin, "Fara," in *OEANE* 2, 301–3.

110. Lambert and Millard, *Atra-Ḥasis*, 11.

111. Translations in Lambert and Millard, *Atra-Ḥasis*, 42–125 and Benjamin Foster, "*Atra-Ḥasis*," in *COS* 1:450–53.

112. Lambert and Millard, *Atra-Ḥasis*, 57.

Before twelve hundred years had passed, the human population had grown and the human masses made too much noise:[113]

> the gods got disturbed with [their uproar]
> [Enlil heard] their noise
> [And addressed] the great gods,
>> "The noise of mankind [had become too intense for me],
>> [With their uproar] I am deprived of sleep."

The gods determined to bring a flood on the earth in order to rid the earth of noisy humanity. As was the case in the Gilgamesh flood story, Enki double-crossed the divine assembly and informed Atrahasis, who reverenced Enki and regularly prayed to him.[114]

Tablet III of the epic records instructions to build a boat, prescriptions that closely parallel those found in the Gilgamesh version. What the Atrahasis version adds to the other accounts is the creation of humans, how they made the gods angry, and how the flood was intended to eliminate the divine dilemma. Since the Gilgamesh flood story probably derived from Atrahasis, it is not surprising that the details of the flood and the aftermath are virtually identical. Similarly, the deities in both welcome the food and drink offerings after the flood. As is reported in Gilgamesh, in Atrahasis the gods "gather like flies over the offering."

The New "Ark Tablet"

In 2014, Irving Finkel published the text of a cuneiform tablet that he had briefly examined in 1985 that was owned by a private individual.[115] Only in 2009 did the owner allow Finkel sufficient access to the tablet that allowed him to decipher and translate what he has now dubbed "the Ark tablet." Written in Akkadian between 1900 and 1700 BC, this tablet is a copy of a larger and older text tradition, Finkel opines. It begins with the divine speech (by Enki?) to Atrahasis to demolish his reed house and build a boat.[116] The boat was to be circular in shape, a detail strikingly different from all other textual traditions. The tale

---

113. Ibid., 67.
114. Ibid., 67–69.
115. Finkel, *The Ark Before Noah*, 106.
116. For a translation of the entire text, see Ibid., 107–10.

ends with Atrahasis and family on board the boat with the door shut and caulked. Obviously there were tablets that preceded and followed this one, but they have not been found.

The author's study of circular reed boats, known as coracles, and their use in Mesopotamia from most ancient to recent times is fascinating.[117] His attempts to synthesize the Genesis flood story with this new text and the Babylonian floods stories is, however, not compelling (see next section).

The Hebrew (Biblical) Tradition (Gen 6:9 - 17)

Gunkel held that the "tradition of the Flood in Israel is very ancient," but that "the current form of the legend belongs in a relatively younger time."[118] He also thought that the flood tradition itself originated in Babylon — the flood story of the Gilgamesh Epic had only been published about thirty years prior to Gunkel's writing. OT scholars of the late nineteenth and early twentieth centuries, therefore, were inclined to think that Israel simply borrowed the flood story. S.R. Driver confidently asserted that "there can be no doubt that the true origin of the Biblical narrative is to be found in the Babylonian story of the Flood."[119] Driver and other source critics maintained that the Hebrew narrative was made up of two literary traditions, those of the Yahwist (J) and the Priestly (P) writer, which were merged to create a composite narrative.[120]

In his recent investigation of the flood traditions, Finkel appeals to nineteenth-century source critical theories to explain apparent contradictions in the Hebrew version. He describes the Documentary Hypothesis as a "long-established and largely non-contentious branch of biblical scholarship."[121] Regrettably, he seems totally oblivious to the developments in Pentateuchal studies over the past thirty years (see above). Robert Alter's nearly two decades-old assessment of the state

---

117. Ibid., 119–55.

118. Gunkel, *Genesis*, 67.

119. Driver, *The Book of Genesis*, 103.

120. For a more recent advocate of this view, see John Van Seters, *Prologue to History: The Yahwist as Historian in Genesis* (Louisville: Westminster/John Knox Press, 1992), 160–65. Richard Elliott Friedman, *Who Wrote the Bible?* (New York: HarperCollins, 1997), 53–60. Westermann, *Genesis 1–11*, 412–13.

121. Finkel, *The Ark Before Noah*, 194.

of source critical studies of the OT is even more accurate today, and reminds us that it has indeed been contentious. He observes:[122]

> In fact all the details of the Documentary Hypothesis are continually, and often quite vehemently debated ... Enormous energy has been invested in discriminating the precise boundaries between one document and the next ... It is small wonder that the Documentary Hypothesis, whatever its general validity, has begun to look as though it has reached a point of diminishing returns, and many younger scholars, showing signs of restlessness with source criticism, have been exploring other approaches—literary, anthropological, sociological, and so forth—to the Bible.

Finkel then goes so far as to speculate that the differences between the J and P flood narratives in Genesis can be attributed to the Hebrew tradents having access to different versions of the flood tradition.[123] His efforts to explain the Hebrew tradition in light of his important discovery is more creative than convincing.

Let us return to consider how the Genesis flood narrative is presented in the Bible. The story occupies the entirety of the third *tôlĕdôt* in Genesis (6:9–9:28). My treatment above of the *tôlĕdôt* formulae as a genre pertains here. That is why I concur with the translations "this is the history of Noah" (Cassuto)[124] or "this is the family history of Noah" (Wenham),[125] as capturing the essence of the material contained in this unit.

Despite the classic position that the flood story is a literary composite, more recent treatment of the flood narrative has shown the coherence and unity of the story. Wenham's seminal study has shown that the narrative is arranged palistrophically or chiastically, that is, a passage arranged in a verbal pattern that moves towards the turning point or apex ("God remembered Noah"—Gen 8:1) and then, as the story

---

122. Robert Alter, *Genesis: Translation and Commentary* (New York: W.W. Norton & Co., 1996), xi.

123. Finkel, *The Ark Before Noah*, 222–23.

124. Cassuto, *A Commentary of the Book of Genesis*, 2:47.

125. Wenham, *Genesis 1–15*, 169. For a critique of Wenham's structural analysis, see J.A. Emerton, "An Examination of Some Attempts to Defend the Unity of the Flood Narrative in Genesis" *VT* 37 no. 4, part 1 (1988): 401–20, and "An Examination of Some Attempts to Defend the Unity of the Flood Narrative in Genesis" *VT* 38 no. 1, part 2 (1987): 1–21.

moves towards resolution, key words and numbers appear in the same place in the second part of the narrative (8:2–19) as they did in the opening section (6:10–7:24).[126]

A Noah (6:10a)

  B Shem, Ham, and Japheth (10b)

    C Ark to be built (14–16)

      D Flood announced (17)

        E Covenant with Noah (18–20)

          F Food in the ark (21)

            G Command to enter ark (7:1–3)

              H 7 days waiting for flood (4–5)

                I 7 days waiting for flood (7–10)

                  J Entry to ark (11–15)

                    K Yahweh shuts Noah in (16)

                      L 40 days flood (17a)

                        M Waters increase (17b–18)

                          N Mountains covered (19–20)

                            O 150 days waters prevail (21–24)

                              P GOD REMEMBERS NOAH (8:1)

                            O' 150 days waters abate (3)

                        N' Mountain tops visible (4–5)

                      M' Waters abated (5)

                    L' 40 days (end of) (6a)

                K' Noah opens window of ark (6b)

              J' Raven & dove leave ark (7–9)

             I' 7 days waiting for waters to subside (10–11)

          H' 7 days waiting for waters to subside (12–13)

        G' Command to leave ark (15–16 [22])

      F' Food outside ark (9:1–4)

    E' Covenant with all flesh (8–10)

    D' No flood in the future (11–17)

  C' Ark (18a)

  B' Shem, Ham, and Japheth (18b)

A' Noah (19)

126. Gordon Wenham, "The Coherence of the Flood Narrative," *VT* 28 (1978): 336–48. Wenham, *Genesis 1–15*, 155–208.

One notices how the numbers seven, forty, and one hundred and fifty line up beautifully in this analysis, as do other key words. Because the narrative fits so well together, "a marvelous coherent unity,"[127] Wenham suggests that while the two-source hypothesis is plausible, a single source may be behind the flood narrative. Another reason for this conclusion is that the thematic parallels between the so-called J and P sources and Mesopotamian flood narratives, best aligns when they are combined. He observes, "It is strange that two accounts of the flood so different as J and P circulating in ancient Israel, should have been combined to give our present story which has many more resemblances to the Gilgamesh version than the postulated sources."[128]

The basic sequence of events found in the Mesopotamian flood traditions are also found in Genesis 1–11 (with slight variations). Forty years ago Kenneth Kitchen discerned the following parallel motifs:[129]

ATRAHASIS	GENESIS 1–11
(Creation &) Mankind	Creation, includes mankind
Narrative: alienation	Narrative: alienation, genealogy
Flood, new start, mankind	Flood, new start, mankind, genealogy

Isaac Kikiwada and Arthur Quinn embraced Wenham's chiastic analysis of the flood narrative and further argued for structural unity of all of Genesis 1–11 (presaging Rendsburg's monograph cited above).[130] For Kikiwada and Quinn, the structure mirrors the pattern found in the plot sequence in Atrahasis, as recognized by Kitchen.[131] This is the comparative analysis they proposed:[132]

---

127. Wenham, "The Coherence of the Flood Narrative," 348.

128. Ibid., 347.

129. Kenneth Kitchen, *The Bible in Its World* (Exeter: Paternoster Press, 1977), 31–34. Updated and expanded in *The Reliability of the Old Testament* (Grand Rapids: Eerdmans, 2003), 422–28.

130. See Isaac Kikiwada and Arthur Quinn, *Before Abraham Was: A Provocative Challenge to the Documentary Hypothesis* (Nashville: Abingdon, 1985), 45–52, 54–138.

131. These authors do not cite Kitchen's 1977 study, suggesting that they came to similar conclusions independently.

132. Kikiwada and Quinn, *Before Abraham Was*, 47–48.

ATRAHASIS	GENESIS 1 - 11
A. Creation	**A. Creation (1:1 - 2:3)**
Summary of work of gods Creation of man	Summary of work of God Creation of man
B. First threat	**B. First threat (2:4 - 3:24)**
Man's numerical increase Plague, Enki's help	Genealogy of heaven and earth, Adam and Eve
C. Second threat	**C. Second threat (4:1 - 26)**
Man's numerical increase Drought, numerical increase Intensified drought Enki's help	Cain and Abel Cain and Abel, genealogy Lamech's taunt (in genealogy)
D. Final threat	**D. Final threat (Gen 5:2 - 9:29)**
Numerical increase Atrahasis' flood Salvation in boat	Genealogy Noah's flood Salvation in ark
E. Resolution	**E. Resolution**
Numerical increase Compromise Enlil and Enki, "Birth control"	Genealogy Tower of Babel & dispersion genealogy Abram leaves Ur

It is my contention that the similarities in plot sequence between these two traditions is not the result of direct borrowing, as some maintain (and most recently argued by Finkel), but that both stories independently reflect a memory of one and the same event. I also believe that the text of Genesis could well have been written in such a way as to maximally challenge the prevailing Mesopotamian view of things. Kikiwada and Quinn are on point to propose that "Genesis 1–11 is written in opposition to the Mesopotamian Atrahasis traditions."[133]

Noah's story lacks the geographical details of the Eden narrative, but there seems to have been no shift in setting from the general "east of Eden" (Gen 3:24; 4:16) as being Noah's home. The ark does come to rest "on the mountains of Ararat." Hebrew Ararat corresponds to Urartu, a toponym known in Assyrian texts as early as the thirteenth century BC.[134] Urartu is the mountainous region north of ancient Assyria

---

133. Ibid., 52.
134. Paul Zimasnky, "Urartu," in *OEANE* 5, 291–94.

that extends into the Caucasus Mountains. The ark ends up, then, in a geographically recognizable area in northern Mesopotamia. In Genesis 10, the so-called "Table of Nations" contains the genealogies of the sons of Noah (Gen 10:1 — "these are the family histories of the sons of Noah") and the places they settled and the cities they founded. While these are scattered across the ancient Near East, the Levant, Anatolia, and North Africa,[135] the names of Babel, Erech (Uruk), and Calneh[136] in the land of Shinar (10:10) show the centrality of the Tigris-Euphrates Valley in the post flood tradition.

Concluding Thoughts on the Flood Traditions

At every turn in the Mesopotamian flood tradition(s), one can imagine the biblical authors having a good laugh as they read or heard these stories. While Israelites believed that their God, Yahweh, neither slumbers nor sleeps (Ps 121:4), the Babylonian gods in the flood tradition suffered from insomnia because of human noise! The bickering and intrigue among the pantheon must have struck the Hebrew writer and his audience as odd. Then too, the fact that the gods were frightened by the very deluge they had ordained makes them look impotent and foolish, compared with the portrayal of the Hebrew God who controlled his creation, bringing the flood as planned, and then causing a mighty wind (or his spirit, *rûaḥ*) to push back the waters so that the land would dry out (Gen 8:1). Like various Mesopotamian flood heroes, Noah made an offering after disembarking and "the LORD smelled the pleasing aroma" (8:21), but there is no comical depiction of God being hungry and thirsty, craving human sustenance or buzzing around the offering like a famished fly!

The different presentations of deity in the Hebrew and Mesopotamian traditions could not be more striking. Genesis seems aware of the Babylonian versions, and while agreeing that there was a flood, an ark,

---

135. J. Simons, "The 'Table of Nations': Its General Structural Meaning," *Oudtestamentische Studiën* 10 (1954): 155–84, reprinted in Hess & Tsumura, *I Studied Inscriptions from Before the Flood*, 234–53; D. J. Wiseman, Genesis 10: Some Archaeological Considerations," *Faith and Thought* 87 (1955): 14–24, reprinted in Hess & Tsumura, *I Studied Inscriptions from Before the Flood*, 254–69.

136. Probably not a place name, but should be read "all of them" (in Shinar), so Sarna, *Genesis*, 74; Speiser, *Genesis*, 67.

and a survivor, the theological perspective is radically different and is consciously aimed at refuting the Babylonian worldview.

The popular notion that the biblical author(s) borrowed the Babylonian story and appropriated it during the exile in Babylon in the sixth century (an idea renewed recently by Finkel)[137] makes little sense. One might recall the words of the Judean psalmist in Babylon who laments, "By the rivers of Babylon we sat and wept when we remembered Zion" ... "How can we sing the songs of the LORD while in a foreign land?" (Ps 137:1, 4). It is hard to believe that Jewish priests and prophets in Babylon who longed for Zion and felt the shame of being in a foreign land would quickly embrace pagan foreign myths encountered in Babylon and integrate them into their Torah!

Undoubtedly Daniel and his colleagues who were taken to Babylon in 605 BC (Dan 1:1–6) to learn "the language and literature of the Babylonians" (v. 4) encountered versions of the Mesopotamian flood story reviewed above. But here Daniel "resolved not to defile himself with the royal food and wine" (v. 8). Then too, in Daniel 3:18, these same Hebrew men refuse to worship Nebuchanezzar's gold image, declaring, "let it be known to you, O king, that we are not going to serve your gods or worship the golden image that you have set up" (NASB). Are we to believe that Daniel, Hananiah, Mishael, and Azariah (and others like them) would reject food contrary to the Law and refuse to serve Babylonian deities, but would then read the pagan "literature of the Babylonians" and make these stories their own?

It may be that during the Babylonian captivity the existing Noah narrative was tweaked in some way so as to highlight the differences between the Babylonian and Hebrew literary traditions. But, borrowing and adapting the flood story at a time when the Jews, we are told, were trying to record and canonize their history and traditions is hardly the time to borrow a pagan myth.

Lastly, the dominant view of biblical scholars, going back to Wellhausen,[138] is that it was during the exile, when confronted with the polytheism of the region, that monotheism finally took hold within the

---

137. Finkel, *The Ark Before Noah*, 224–60.

138. Julius Wellhausen, *Israelitische und Jüdische Geschichte* (9th ed.; Berlin: de Gruyter, 1958), 29–30, translation in Stephen Cook, *The Social Root of Biblical Yahwism* (Atlanta: Society of Biblical Literature, 2004), 4.

Jewish community. Thus, Israel's monotheism developed in harmony with a general spirit of the times, known as the Axial Age theory in the sixth to fifth century BC.[139] If this movement towards monotheism occurred during the Babylonian captivity, a view championed by Finkel,[140] it seems counterintuitive to take the polytheistic mythic literature of Babylon and place it into the Hebrew monotheistic writings!

Given the Mesopotamian origins of Abraham and his ancestors (Gen 10 and 11:10–32), it should not surprise us that the flood story should be part of the shared memory of the Israelites and the Babylonians.

The Tower of Babel Story (Gen 11:1–9)

Throughout the Table of Nations in Genesis 10, we are introduced to the descendants of the sons of Noah, Japeth, Ham, and Shem and three times the expression, "these are the sons of X by their clans and languages, in their territories" (Gen 10:4, 20, 31) occurs. The phrase raises the question, when did humans start speaking different languages? The narrative of the tower building immediately follows and was intended to answer this question (even though Gen 11 stands within the fourth *tôlēdôt* section that began in 10:1).

Stories that explain the origin of a practice or institution are often called etiologies. Etiologies, however, are not necessarily fictitious accounts. Millard has demonstrated that etiologies are "descriptive" and may or may not be historical, while pointing to etiological stories that have no historical base and to others that reflect reality.[141] Referring to Gen 11 as an etiological story that explains how different languages came about does not mean that the story is imaginary. Etiology, then, speaks more to the function of the story than its literary form.

Cassuto believed that the story itself may have been etiological originally, but its use in the Torah is more theological.[142] For Gunkel,

---

139. Karl Woschitz, "Axial Age," *Religion Past and Present* Vol. 1 (ed. H.D. Betz, et al.; Leiden: Brill, 2007), 531. Jan Assmann, *Of God and Gods: Egypt, Israel, and the Rise of Monotheism* (Madison: University of Wisconsin, 2008), 76–78.

140. Finkel, *The Ark Before Noah*, 239–46.

141. A.R. Millard, "Story, History and Theology," in *Faith, Tradition and History: Old Testament Historiography in its Near Eastern Context* (eds. A.R. Millard, J.K. Hoffmeier & D.W. Baker; Winona Lake: Eisenbrauns, 1994), 40–42.

142. Cassuto, *Genesis*, 2:225.

the tower story is a legend that "explains the origin of the various languages."[143] George Coats considered the Babel narrative to be a "tale," that is a "short narrative."[144]

Not surprisingly, this story too is situated in Babylonia. The tower builders migrated to central Mesopotamia, Shinar specifically. If this narrative picks up after the flood in Chapter 9, then it seems that the movement described in Gen 11:1 was from the Ararat (Urartu) region, so suggests Sarna.[145] If this scenario is correct then the people could well be returning to their ante-diluvial homeland, and, although the text does not specifically say why, they feared being scattered and the tower would help prevent that, then perhaps the memory of the flood in the not so distant past prompted their anxiety.

The etymology of Shinar remains problematic. Early on, scholars thought it might be connected with the word Sumer.[146] Hans Güterbock proposed that the Hebrew word *šin'ār* derives from a Hurrian (Syrian) writing for the word Sumer.[147] An alternative proposal is that the cuneiform word *samharû* stands behind Hebrew *šin'ār* and it is the name of a Kassite tribe.[148] Regardless of the origin of the term, there is no doubt that Shinar refers to an area of central Iraq as Gen 10:10 confirms. The heart of Nimrod's kingdom, in fact, included Babel (Babylon), Erech (Uruk), Akkad (Agade), and Calneh (i.e. all of them) in Shinar.

The Hebrew word *bālal*, meaning confuse[149] (Gen 11:7, 9), sounds similar to *bābel*, making this a wonderful wordplay. The Akkadian name, *bāb-ili*, meaning "gate of God," stands behind the translation Babel.[150] Based on textual evidence, the name Babylon goes back to the twenty-third century BC, though the city grew in prominence during the Amorite period (after 2000 BC), and became the dominant city of the region under the great Hammurabi (eighteenth century BC).[151]

---

143. Gunkel, *Genesis*, 99.

144. Coats, *Genesis*, 94–95; for his definition of tale see 7–8.

145. Sarna, *Genesis*, 81.

146. Delitzsch, *Genesis*, 348. Driver, *Genesis*, 121.

147. Hans Güterbock, "Sargon of Akkad mentioned by Ḫattušili of Hatti," *Journal of Cuneiform Studies* 18 (1964): 1–6, esp. 3.

148. Ron Zadok, "The Origins of the Name of Shinar," *Zeitschrift Assyriologie* 74 (1984): 240–44.

149. KBL 1:134.

150. Evelyn Klengel-Brandt, "Babylon," in *OEANE* 1, 251.

151. Ibid., 251, 254.

Babylon was famous for its grand temple to Marduk, called *esagila*, a Sumerian name that means "structure with upraised head."[152] Its dominant ziggurat has given rise to generations of scholars who maintain that there must be a connection between this pyramid-like temple and the tower in the Hebrew tradition. The Hebrew word rendered "tower" in the Genesis narrative is *migdāl*, normally referring to a defense structure or a lookout,[153] and not a term associated with a temple. So the connection of the tower of Gen 11 and temple or ziggurat in Babylon is tenuous.

There is a Sumerian tradition that recalls a "golden" age when wild animals and scorpions did not exist in the land and humans spoke the same language, "harmony-tongued (?) Sumer."[154] Then, for reasons that are not stated, Enki, god of wisdom, "changed the speech in their mouths, [brought(?)] contention into it, into the speech of man that (until then) had been one."[155] Samuel Noah Kramer, the Sumerologist who translated this text, optimistically declared that this text (only published in 1968) "puts it beyond all doubt that the Sumerians believed that there was a time when all mankind spoke one and the same language," just like in Gen 11.[156] Some Assyriologists have questioned Kramer's view that this text looks back to a blissful past, but rather that it was anticipating some future age.[157]

If we allow that this text, "Enmerkar and the Lord of Aratta," retains a memory of humans speaking one language, followed by divine intervention that confused their tongues (though there is no tower, or temple building associated with the divine action), then it is possible to propose that both the Sumerians and Gen 11 preserve a common memory of a world unified by one language.

---

152. Speiser, *Genesis*, 75–76.

153. KBL 1:543–44. On the defensive nature of this term when associated with place-names across the Levant, see Aaron Burke, "Magdaluma, Migdalim, and Majdil: The Historical Geography and Archaeology of the Magdalua (Migdol)," *BASOR* 346 (2007): 29–57.

154. Samuel Noah Kramer, "The 'Babel of Tongues': A Sumerian Version," *JAOS* 88 (1968): 109.

155. Ibid., 111.

156. Ibid.

157. B. Alster, "An Aspect of 'Enmerkar and the Lord of Aratta," *Revue d'Assyriologie* 67 (1973): 101–9. Thorkild Jacobsen's translation (*COS* 1:547–48), however, treats this confusion of the tongues as being a past event.

Concluding Thoughts

I have argued that the three episodes considered here, like the entirety of the book of Genesis, fit into a literary genre based on the heading to the eleven sections of the book, "this is/these are the histories of X," the *tôlēdôt* formula. Within these units, different literary genres might be used. Regardless of what those might be, the general tenor of the book, and Gen 1–11 in particular, is intended to be thought of as describing real events. A piece of ancient literature concerning past events does not have to be recorded with the kind of historiographical precision that would be expected of a modern academic historian or journalist. The geographical clues provided in Gen 1–11 suggest that these events from the ancient past occurred in the Tigris-Euphrates Valley, in a real world, a world recognizable to the ancient reader or hearer of the narratives. When we consider the framing of the books with the *tôlēdôt* markers and the rather specific geographical settings, which I believe would lead an ancient audience to consider the Nephilim episode, the flood, and Tower of Babel narratives as historical events, then there are good reasons to read these texts this way even in the twenty-first century.

Based on this well-founded assumption, biblical theology begins its task. Like the Psalmists of old, Christian theology is founded on God's "glorious deeds ... the wonders that he has done" (Ps 78:4) and we set our "hope in God and not forget the works of God" (Ps 78:7). If one reduces the narratives of Gen 1–11 to fictitious stories and legends, the history of salvation lacks its *raison d'être*. Fortunately, the Christian committed to Scripture need not commit intellectual suicide by embracing the historicity of the events described in early Genesis, for the text itself is written in such a way to reinforce this view.

RESPONSE TO JAMES K. HOFFMEIER

GORDON J. WENHAM

The format of this series demands that each contributor not only expound his own position but also comment on the views of the other contributors. This procedure is liable to highlight the differences between us rather than our points of agreement. So I think it is necessary to state at the outset that, having read my fellow authors' contributions, in our understanding of the message of Gen 1–11 we are in substantial agreement. I am not saying that it does not matter which of our views is preferable, but that we all agree on the picture of God and his relationship to his creation that these chapters portray. On the one hand, none of us is defending an extreme literalist view that requires us to regard the days of Gen 1 as 24 hours long, or like Jewish tradition and Archbishop Ussher use the ages of the patriarchs to establish the date of creation. On the other hand, none of us holds that these chapters are just fiction, that is, tales based solely on the imagination of some ancient Israelite. We are all somewhere in between. We all hold that these narratives reflect real events, yet we believe that they should not be interpreted as though they were written by a twenty-first-century journalist or historian. Rather we need to recover the mindset of the ancient author by situating his account within the culture with which he was familiar.

James Hoffmeier, as an Egyptologist of repute, knows more about the culture of the ancient Near East than either I or Kenton Sparks, and it shows in his contribution, which is packed full of cross-references to sources parallel to or different from the material in Genesis. After reviewing some critical theories about the composition of Genesis, he mentions the importance of genealogies in the ancient Orient, observing that their validity depends on those listed being understood as historical. Then he points to the geographical details in Gen 2:10–14, identifying the rivers flowing out of Eden including the Tigris and the Euphrates. This shows that Eden for the author was a real place, not a paradisial make-believe. Similarly, the account of the divine-human hybrids, the Nephilim, in Gen 6:1–4 has its analogy in ancient thinking: heroic kings known to be historical are sometimes said to be of hybrid parentage. This shows that the ancients at least would not have dismissed Gen 6:1–4 as fiction. The flood story was also very well known in the ancient Near East: many mostly fragmentary copies of this story have been discovered, so its retelling in Genesis is no surprise. But Hoffmeier points out that the flood hero in one version was the son of a famous king, while the ark landed on a known mountain. This links the flood story with places that were familiar to ancient storytellers and their listeners. Finally, the Tower of Babel story has links with an ancient Sumerian tale about all peoples once speaking the same language. Thus Hoffmeier concludes: "Gen 1–11 in particular is intended to be thought of as describing real events" (p. 58).

So far so good. I find myself in substantial agreement with Hoffmeier's conclusion. But I am less sure about some of the arguments that he appeals to in support of his conclusion. Hoffmeier, and also Sparks, spend a lot of time discussing the main critical theories about the composition of these chapters. Hoffmeier aims to refute these theories, while Sparks is happy to endorse them albeit using his own terminology for the writers (J = antiquarian, P = apologist, R(edactor) = anthologist). Having spent much of my career debating these theories, I find myself much closer to Hoffmeier than to Sparks on this issue. The standard Documentary Hypothesis (JEDP) is much too complex to be credible. Indeed though the flood story is one of the parade examples for documentary analysis, I have argued that an essentially unitary reading is more plausible.[158] I have suggested that a much simplified documentary hypothesis, like that favored in the pre-Wellhausen era, has more to commend it.[159]

But whatever source theory is right, how Gen 1–11 was compiled is, I believe, irrelevant in determining the present genre of Gen 1–11. This

158. Gordon J. Wenham, "The Coherence of the Flood Narrative," *VT* 28 (1978): 336–48; Gordon J. Wenham, "Method in Pentateuchal Source Criticism," *VT* 41 (1991):84–109.
159. Gordon J. Wenham, "The Priority of P," *VT* 49 (1999): 240–58.

is true of any composition or work of art. It is not the artist's palette that determines whether the final picture is a portrait or a still life. It is not whether an author borrows his ideas from the classics or from his own experience that determines whether his book turns out to be a romance or a detective story. In both cases it is the arrangement of the material in the end product that determines whether we call it a portrait or still life, a romance or detective story.

The same is true in Gen 1–11. It is irrelevant whether ancient Israelites learned about the flood from the Babylonians or the Phoenicians, whether Abraham knew about it because he grew up in Ur, or that Moses learned about it at the Egyptian court. Similarly its date of composition is irrelevant whether it entered Scripture in the early second millennium (so probably Hoffmeier) or in the fifth century BC (so probably Sparks). The message is the same in either case. In my opinion, both Hoffmeier and Sparks spend too long examining the components of Gen 1–11 and too little time in contemplating the final product. Ancient Near Eastern parallels to Gen 1–11 have their value in helping us to see what is distinctive about Genesis, just as looking at pictures by Rembrandt's contemporaries helps us to appreciate his works better. But ultimately each picture must be evaluated on its own terms.

The same holds for the stories in Gen 1–11. Comparing them with Babylonian accounts of the distant past makes us see more clearly the character of the sovereign Creator, who cares for mankind. These truths are evident without appeal to the parallels. For instance, God's sovereignty is revealed in his first command, "Let there be light," but the impact of this belief would be more striking in a culture where gods depended on man for food, fought each other, and cowered like dogs in the face of the flood. So, while looking at parallels to the biblical account has its value, we need to reflect on the whole final product to grasp what it is trying to convey.

In my view, the book of Genesis is a genealogy with digressions or expansions focusing on key episodes or actors in the story. Each new section of the book has the heading, "These are the generations of (name of patriarch)." Sometimes just a brief genealogy follows (5:1; 25:12; 36:1); sometimes a lengthy account about a particular family (2:4, Adam's offspring; 6:9, Noah's family). Sternberg[160] has pointed out that what determines whether a story should be regarded as historical or fictional is not its form but the intention of the author. Just think of the debates about Job or Jonah. Is the book of Jonah a parable or a historical report? It makes the same point about God's compassion whether it is historical or parabolic. Sternberg argues that if a text contains inaccuracies that does not necessarily make it unhistorical, only bad history. What determines whether a text should be classified as history or something else depends on the intentions of the writer. In the case of Jonah, was the writer, like Nathan or Jesus in their parables, just making a point, or was there a real prophet called Jonah or an actual Good Samaritan?

Applying this criterion of authorial purpose to Gen 1–11, Hoffmeier has pointed to some features, notably the *tôlēdôt* formulae ("These are the generations of ..."), which imply that the writer had an interest in history. But as I have argued in my essay, I think we need a more nuanced characterization of the genre of Genesis, which I termed protohistory. Otherwise, we may be forced to conclude that Genesis is trying to relate history but not succeeding, which would be a rather negative conclusion.

---

160. Meir Sternberg, *The Poetics of Biblical Narrative* (Bloomington: Indiana University Press, 1985), 23–34.

RESPONSE TO JAMES K. HOFFMEIER

KENTON L. SPARKS

Dr. Hoffmeier's essay represents well an approach to the early chapters of Genesis that predominates within the conservative wing of evangelical biblical scholarship and, for this reason, is a fitting and welcome contribution to this "three views" book. Of the three contributors, he is less willing than I or Dr. Wenham to embrace commonly accepted scholarly views of the composition and genres of Gen 1–11. It is fair to say that I am, of the three, most willing to accept these views, though it is not always clear how much space there is between my views and those of Wenham. I'll take up that issue in my response to him.

As for Dr. Hoffmeier, I would like to engage his essay by distilling and responding to the various theses that he develops in the piece. Because his basic points (as I see them) are not always in discrete sections of his discussion, my rubric for the engagement does not follow precisely the order of his paper. I hope that my discussion fairly represents his perspectives and apologize in advance for any misunderstandings.

Hoffmeier Thesis 1: Myth in the technical sense is concerned with ultimate realities, not fiction. The author of the creation stories in Genesis used ancient mythical imagery and language to depict the actual events of history. If an event is narrated in Genesis, in some form or fashion, it happened as narrated.

Our generic categories should be derived from the *actual texts* we are studying and not invented apart from and then foisted upon the texts.[161] In the present case, the ancient texts that are most similar to the early chapters of Genesis—such as *Enuma Elish*, Atrahasis and Adapa—were certainly written using fictional modes of composition, so these

---

161. See my opening essay, where I discuss the difference between generic realism and nominalism.

cannot fit into Hoffmeier's definition of myth because he explicitly excludes "fiction" from the category.[162] This in itself suggests that his category is not useful. Hoffmeier's generic confusion is further compounded by unconscious sleight of hand, in that he artificially conflates the representation of "ultimate reality" with non-fiction, as if fiction cannot represent reality.[163] Reality can and often is represented through fiction, as we see in the parables of Jesus and the trilogies of C. S. Lewis.

Even if we ignore these theoretical slips and try as best we can to accept Hoffmeier on his own terms, significant questions remain. If the author of Genesis used mythical imagery, as Hoffmeier has suggested, then which images are mythic symbol and which are closer to historical representation? Does Hoffmeier believe that the cosmos was created in six literal days? Does he believe that the first woman was made from Adam's rib? Does he believe that a serpent spoke in the garden? Does he believe that our broken human condition can be traced back to eating pieces of fruit? Does he believe in giants who roamed the pre-flood earth? Does he believe in a literal world-wide flood, and a boat with animals? Does he believe that God created rainbows to remind himself not to destroy us again? And how does all of this relate to what is now public knowledge about human origins, which emerged over millions of years through a long evolutionary process rather than in one literal day? One wonders why Hoffmeier does not answer these questions when the historicity of Gen 1–11 is the main theme of our discussion.

Hoffmeier Thesis 2: The tôlēdôt structure of Genesis, with its families and genealogies, provides the basic structure of the book. These genealogies parallel those from elsewhere in the ancient Near East and share with them a historical purpose. From this we may infer that the author of Genesis intended to write a narrative about the lives of actual historical persons.

Hoffmeier recognizes the obvious parallels between the genealogies of Genesis and those from the ancient world but errs when he infers

---

162. Space does not permit me to tease out the subtle relationships between history and fiction, but I should point out that fictional (i.e., creative) modes of narrative composition do not necessarily exclude historical purpose (authors may believe their fictions), but fiction does necessarily exclude accurate historical results (because created stories cannot map closely to historical events).

163. This is a common error in conservative evangelical theology, as I mentioned in my opening essay.

from this the historical accuracy of the genealogies in Gen 1–11. The comparative texts reveal that ancient genealogies were very poor witnesses to early human history, this for the obvious reason that no one was around to record and preserve the genealogical records. The Assyrian King List (AKL), which Hoffmeier surprisingly cites as an example, resorts to tribal eponyms in the earliest parts of the genealogy because these were taken from an earlier Amorite tribal genealogy.[164] This section of AKL is similar to the "Table of Nations" in Gen 10, which also uses eponyms to account for the origins of various nations and peoples. Generically closer to the biblical "Table" is the Hesiodic "Catalogue of Women," which traces the origins of each nation and people carefully back to a forefather of the same name.[165] We may learn a great deal about social history and ethnic boundaries from these genealogies, but they've little to tell us about the actual origins of nations and peoples.

As for the linear genealogies in Gen 5 and 11, these are most similar to the Sumerian King List (SKL), which like Genesis bestows long lifespans on heroes who lived before and after the great flood. Some or many of SKL's heroic kings may have been historical persons, but as a source of early human history the list presents many problems. According to the SKL, cities and kings emerged immediately after the gods created humanity, and kingship itself is understood as a single institution that allowed for only one legitimate dynasty at a time. None of this works as genuine history because neither the cities listed, nor their kings, emerged soon after human life evolved, and the various dynasties did not arise one after another but often as contemporary political developments. Needless to say, the very long reigns attributed to these kings do not reflect their actual lifespans.

Setting to one side Hoffmeier's oversights respecting the comparative material, it seems to me that the deeper problem in his thesis is theoretical. Hoffmeier assumes throughout his essay that an author's "historical intention" must yield "historical accuracy." Why should we

---

164. See a discussion of this text, and the closely related "Genealogy of Hammurabi's Dynasty," in Sparks, *ATSHB*, 349–50, 355.

165. The "Catalogue" is a long Greek historical text that uses genealogies to connect various traditions into a larger narrative whole. For more on the text itself, see my essay in this volume and M. L. West, *The Hesiodic Catalogue of Women: Its Nature, Structure, and Origins* (Oxford: Oxford University Press, 1985); Sparks, *ATSHB*, 356-57.

assume this? The accuracy of a historical writer depends not on his/her good intentions but rather on the quality of the sources consulted. And from what we find in Genesis and similar ancient Near Eastern texts, it is clear that the authors did not have access to dependable historical sources for the earliest periods of human existence.

Hoffmeier Thesis 3: The author of Genesis situates the Edenic Garden within geographical spaces familiar to the ancient audience. From this we may infer that the author intended to narrate actual historical events within a concrete historical context.

As I said in my response to Thesis 2, the historical intentions of the biblical author by no means ensure historical accuracy, for accuracy depends on the author's sources rather than on intentions. Even if one or more authors of Gen 1–11 were historians who wrote on the basis of other documentary sources, it is clear that the sources were largely "mythical" (that is, similar to texts such as *Enuma Elish*, Atrahasis and Adapa) and were not accurate historical reports. Moreover, we do well to remember that ancient historians sometimes used fictional modes of composition to introduce new ideas and themes into what was ostensibly source-based history.[166] The notion of generic purity, which imagines that ancient historians were "handcuffed" by their sources and could never invent any stories for themselves, stands very far from the generic realities of ancient historiography and of ancient writing in general.

One final point: Hoffmeier argues that the four rivers of paradise (Tigris, Euphrates, Pishon, and Gihon) were known to the ancient audience and hence pointed to a literal, concrete location for the Edenic garden. However, he also argues that the Pishon was the so-called "Kuwait River," which dried up centuries before Israel existed and of which the Genesis author is somehow aware. Hoffmeier finds it "remarkable indeed" that the author knows about this ancient river, by which he means (as near as I can tell) that the river's existence was revealed to the author by God. My question is: Shall I believe, as Hoffmeier has argued, that the author spoke of things known to the ancient audience to show them (and us) that Eden was historical, or shall we now follow Hoffmeier in rejecting this thesis because only the author,

---

166. For the influence of creative invention in historiography, see Sparks, *ATSHB*, 361–416, esp. 410–11.

and not the audience, knew of the long-lost Pishon River? One cannot have it both ways.

Hoffmeier Thesis 4: The episode in Gen 6:1–4, where the "sons of god" cohabit with the "daughters of men," comes as close to myth as anything in Genesis. Although the "sons of god" are often interpreted as fallen heavenly beings, in part because they (or their children) are called Nephilim (from the Hebrew word for "fall"), this view is wanting because the term něfilîm is not a passive verbal form and so cannot refer to "fallen" beings. Therefore, Gen 6:1–4 is not mythical. Rather, it "demythologizes" an ancient myth which the biblical author inherited from his Near Eastern context. Furthermore, this ancient myth was itself a mythicized version of an actual historical event that incited God to send the great flood.

As near as I can tell, Hoffmeier believes that the "sons of God" episode in Gen 6 preserves an account of the actual historical events that caused the great flood. He further believes that this primal story was subsequently "mythicized" in the ancient Near Eastern tradition before the author of Genesis adopted and "demythed" the story, presumably because the author did not like myths. I find this argument quite odd (and needlessly complex), but the more pressing issue for me, as a reader, is Hoffmeier's stance on the historicity of Gen 6:1–4. His description of the story seems to vacillate subtly between "myth" and "demythed myth," such that I cannot discern with any confidence which elements in the story reflect mythical representation and which reflect historical representation. What, precisely, has the biblical author "demythed?" After all, the Bible reports that supernatural "sons of god" caroused with and beget powerful children through human women. As I see it, that's pretty mythical.

One of Hoffmeier's central arguments in this part of his essay fails because (as near as I can tell) he has misunderstood Hebrew grammar. According to Hoffmeier, the Nephilim in Gen 6 cannot be "fallen ones" (i.e., fallen heavenly beings) because the linguistic form is not a "passive." He seems to believe that a passive is needed to render this meaning, and that its absence somehow means that něfilîm cannot refer to fallen heavenly beings. This, in turn, suggests that the text is less "mythical" than usually assumed.

The difficulty with this argument is that in Hebrew, as in English, the verb "to fall" (*nāfal*) is never used in passive voice because the action (falling) is already happening to the subject. Moreover, it turns out that *něfilîm* is a substantive based on the same verbal root and, though the verb does not take a passive form, this substantive indeed follows a passive structure, as noted by Hendel.[167] So a proper reading would be "fallen ones," in spite of the fact that Hoffmeier claims this cannot be right.[168] As I see it, the mythical interpretation for this text—that it refers to divine beings cohabiting with human women—remains the best one. Wenham, the other contributor to this volume, agrees with me on this point.

Hoffmeier Thesis 5: Similarities between the biblical and ancient Near Eastern flood stories are not the result of direct borrowing but reflect instead competing memories of the same historical event. This implies, of course, that the great flood actually did take place at some point in early human history.

There are two significant problems with this thesis, one historical and the other scientific. On the historical front, Hoffmeier's argument seems inconsistent, for he admits that the biblical flood story was written long after and as a response to Near Eastern versions of the tale.[169] Given that the Israelite version *responds* to the Mesopotamian versions, we must suppose that the biblical authors read and were influenced deeply by the earlier flood stories. So the borrowing was quite direct, however much the biblical authors edited and rearranged the tradition. On the scientific front, the biblical and Near Eastern flood stories *cannot* reflect different but accurate memories of the same event because a world-wide flood with boat and animals, as described in the tales, simply did not take place. The biological and geological evidence on hand does not square remotely with the claim that all living things, save those on a giant boat, were once saved from a great flood. Honestly, I wish for the sake of ease that the evidence were otherwise ...

---

167. The *qatil* adjectival form. See Ronald S. Hendel, "Of Demigods and the Deluge: Toward an Interpretation of Genesis 6:1–4," *JBL* 106 (1987): 13–26; cf. Wilhelm Gesenius, *Genesius' Hebrew Grammar* (2nd English ed.; ed. E. Kautzch and A. E. Cowley; Oxford: Clarendon, 1985), 231.

168. I suspect that the term *něfilîm* is already a proper noun in Genesis, so the best translation may well be "Nephilim." But the etymological origins and development of the word would still be as I've described.

169. Hoffmeier: "to maximally challenge the prevailing Mesopotamian view of things."

but it is not. Perhaps there was once a great but more modest flood that inspired these Near Eastern traditions, but this "local flood" would not have endangered all living things, which is a central theme in all of the ancient flood stories.

Hoffmeier Thesis 6: The episode at Babel, in Gen 11, reports that humanity spoke a single language until God intervened to create many languages. Because the Sumerians also knew of this tradition, the two testimonies together imply that the biblical report is historically accurate.

Hoffmeier would be hard pressed to defend his historical assertion that languages were created all at once. The evidence on hand suggests instead that each language develops from earlier languages through a process of linguistic evolution. Thus, for example, Italian, French, and Spanish are developments of the Latin language. So why does the Bible suggest otherwise?

Ancient peoples like the Sumerians and Israelites did not understand linguistic evolution and so invented etiologies to explain the mysterious diversity of language. According to the Israelite etiology, humanity's one and only language was Hebrew until God intervened to create other languages, which are presumably enumerated in the lists of Genesis chapter 10.[170] But Hebrew was not the first human language, nor did the languages listed in Gen 10 (such as Egyptian) appear suddenly as through a miracle. Linguistic evolution is the better explanation. So the Babel episode, while culturally fascinating and sociologically illuminating, does not offer dependable linguistic history. The Israelites bear no more fault for this misunderstanding than did Newton for overlooking quantum physics. They were people of their times. But their Babel story depicted well, and still depicts well, the dark and broken arrogance of humanity.

Hoffmeier Thesis 7: Although biblical scholarship once believed that discrete sources, written by different authors and editors, stood behind the book of Genesis, this old view is misguided because (a) recent biblical scholarship has roundly challenged the old source-theories of Genesis, and (b) there is good evidence within Genesis itself that it was written or shaped by a single

---

170. See Jub 3:28; 12:25–27; Josephus, *Ant.* I.117–18; Rashi's commentary on Gen 2:23 and 11:1 in *The Metsudah Chumash* (trans. A. Davis; Hoboken, NJ: KTAV, 1991) 29, 105.

author. Therefore, the hypothetical sources behind Genesis can be ignored in our generic analysis of Gen 1–11.

My own essay accentuates the generic importance of the sources and compositions that shaped the book of Genesis. While knowledge of and appreciation for these sources is not necessary for a good reading of Genesis, the existence of these sources *is* important—vital, in fact—for the *historical* questions we were tasked to address in this book. Obviously, when we have two or more conflicting versions of the same story, one or both cannot be historically accurate.

While I am not surprised that Hoffmeier rejects my source-sensitive approach, I am somewhat (but not wholly) surprised by the evidence he uses to make his case against it. Hoffmeier cites several modern scholars who, he believes, provide support for his view that Genesis is a single, coherent narrative written by one person. The modern sources include two collections of essays edited respectively by Dozeman/Schmid and Dozeman/Schmid/Römer, and several books and essays by Jack Sasson, Gary Rendsburg, Robert Alter, and Kikawada/Quinn. I am quite familiar with all of these scholars and can say with confidence that, in every case, the author stands entirely against Hoffmeier's view or has nothing to offer in favor of it.

Contributors to the two collections of essays (Dozeman/Schmid and Dozeman/Schmid/Römer) are first-rate scholars. And without exception, each essay assumes the existence of the various source profiles in the Pentateuch, including (at least) P, D, and non-P (or J). Not a single contributor holds that Genesis was written by a single person, let alone Moses. As for Jack Sasson, with whom I studied and for whom I served for several years as a teaching and research assistant, he is hardly sympathetic with Hoffmeier's cause. Sasson's article argues for an overarching *redactional* (editorial) unity, not a simple authorial unity. Lest he be misunderstood as denying the underlying sources of the Pentateuch, Sasson writes: "At the outset, therefore, I should state that … it is entirely proper for scholarship to concern itself with the origins and significance of each one of the many units that are identified in the OT." Robert Alter offers even less support for Hoffmeier, for he not only accepts the standard three-source hypothesis for Genesis (J, E, P) but also describes the biblical narrative as "fiction." It's quite true that

Alter wants to push readers beyond the sources so that the overall poetic and artistic unity of Genesis can be appreciated, but when commenting on *history* he honors the sources by referring to this unity as "composite artistry."[171]

Rendsburg and Kikawada/Quinn may appear more sympathetic with Hoffmeier's agenda, but any similarities are quite superficial. Although Rendsburg postulates that a single editor compiled the book of Genesis, the resulting unity is redactional only and does not yield a seamless story. He admits that stark evidence of the editor's diverse and contrary sources remains in the biblical text.[172] Kikawada and Quinn take the next step by describing the writer as an *author* (rather than an editor), but they likewise admit that the results are inconsistent and contradictory, largely because ancient authors did not care about these contradictions.[173] Hoffmeier's "Genesis" is something altogether different. It is a single coherent book, written by one author (Moses), which contains no contradictory perspectives and is essentially (if not wholly) accurate as a book of history. If Hoffmeier is seeking academic allies to support this perspective, he will have to look elsewhere.

Does Professor Wenham, another contributor to this volume, fit the bill? Hoffmeier seems to think so. I'll discuss this in more detail in my response to Wenham.

Conclusions

What is the generic character of early chapters of Genesis, and what implications does this have for the historicity of the events narrated therein? As I understand it, these are the key questions our book addresses. While I do not agree, generally, with Dr. Hoffmeier's construal of the evidence, nor with his fundamental conclusions, in the end we do agree on two points. First, we believe that one or more authors of Genesis wrote of events that were considered historical by the ancient audience, the great flood being an obvious example. Secondly, we *seem*

---

171. See ch. 7 of Robert Alter, *The Art of Biblical Narrative* (New and rev. ed.; New York: Basic Books, 2011), 163–92.

172. I thank Dr. Rendsburg for confirming this via email.

173. See, for example, their discussion of contradictory genealogies in Isaac M. Kikawada and Arther Quinn, *Before Abraham Was: The Unity of Genesis 1–11* (Nashville, Abingdon Press, 1985), 58–59.

to agree that some elements of Gen 1–11 were not written as straight-forward history but rather by drawing on images from what is usually called "myth." I have suggested that this combination of historical intent and mythical content stems from the generic character of Genesis, to wit, that it was written by two ancient historians who drew upon many sources, some of them mythical and legendary, and who also composed their own stories to imbue the whole with a theological message. The two histories were finally combined by an editor who was more inter-ested in preserving the two voices than in meeting our modern expecta-tions for historical and theological coherence.

Hoffmeier and I differ most starkly, I think, in our respective engagements with the "elephant in the room," namely, the external evidence which bears on the historicity of Genesis. That the biblical authors sought (more or less) to narrate history is a different thing from getting that history right. And the comparative generic evidence sug-gests that they were not drawing on foolproof historical sources, while the scientific evidence (biological, geological, anthropological, linguis-tic) makes clear that, in the end, most of Gen 1–11 simply *cannot* be accurate history. Hoffmeier hints at points that he knows Genesis can-not be straightforward history in every detail, but he meticulously avoids admitting that anything narrated in Genesis did not happen as narrated.

CHAPTER TWO

GENESIS 1 – 11 AS PROTOHISTORY

GORDON J. WENHAM

The book of Genesis contains a variety of literary types. There are genealogies, a king list, poems both short and long, and narrative material. Naming the genre of these different elements is not easy, especially when it comes to the opening chapters 1–11. Here we have several genealogies: 4:17–22 of Cain, 4:25–26 and 5:1–32 of Seth, 11:10-32 of Shem. Whether the Table of Nations of chapter 10 is really a genealogy is not clear, but its title is similar to that of the other genealogies in chapters 5 and 11. The definition of poetry is difficult, but Adam's exclamation on meeting Eve in 2:23 is poetic if not poetry, as is Lamech's vengeance-filled boast to his wives in 4:23–24. God's curses on Adam, Eve, and the serpent in 3:14–19 could be classed as poetry, and some have held that 1:1–2:3 is poetry too.

But it is the rest of the material in chapters 2–11 that is really hard to classify. What should we call the stories of Adam and Eve or the account of Noah and the flood? Westermann[1] simply terms them narrative, which is a safe definition, but the modern reader would like more precision. Is it history, myth or fiction, or is it *sui generis,* a unique type of literature not attested elsewhere? Answering this question requires us to adopt a viewpoint. Are we looking for the view of the original author, how he understood these stories, an *emic* approach? Or are we looking for a definition of their genre in modern categories, an *etic* approach? Much ink has been spilt in these debates and here we are spilling even

---

1. Claus Westermann, *Genesis 1–11: A Commentary* (Minneapolis: Augsburg, 1984), 47–56.

more. But ultimately we must recognize that how we define the genre of Gen 1–11 is a secondary issue: our primary concern must be the interpretation of the stories and their application today. The definition of genre refines and clarifies the message of Genesis, but disagreements about genre should not obscure our substantial agreement about the theological teaching of these stories. Whether one calls Gen 1–11 doctrine, history, fiction, or myth, it is clear that these chapters are making profound statements about the character of God and his relationship to mankind. Elucidating these truths must be the goal of every interpreter.

So how should we proceed? The first aim should be to enter the thought world of the author of Genesis, what is technically called its *cognitive environment*,[2] to see what his presuppositions are and how the Genesis material compares with them. In other words, our aim is an emic approach to these chapters. But this is easier said than done, for discovering the views on origins held in the ancient world when Gen 1–11 was written is highly problematic. Despite the vast number of tablets unearthed and read by Assyriologists, Hittitologists, and Egyptologists, our knowledge of ancient beliefs is patchy. Many of the most relevant texts parallel to Gen 1–11 have gaps at significant places and are not always easy to date. Nor is the composition of Genesis easy to determine: scholars put forward widely different views and no consensus has been reached.[3] But given the very conservative world of the ancient Near East, where traditions were passed on for centuries with little change,[4] these uncertainties have only a limited effect on interpretation and genre assignment. These concerns are further assuaged by focusing on the final form of the texts rather than the putative sources or earlier forms. I shall therefore begin by looking at the smaller literary units within Gen 1–11 before exploring possible definitions of the

2. See John H. Walton, *Genesis 1 as Ancient Cosmology* (Winona Lake: Eisenbrauns, 2011); Daniel D. Lowery, *Toward a Poetics of Genesis 1–11: Reading Genesis 4:17–22 in its Near Eastern Context* (Winona Lake: Eisenbrauns, 2013).

3. See Gordon J. Wenham, *Genesis 1–15: Word Biblical Commentary* (Waco: Word, 1987), xxv–xlv and Wenham, *Exploring the Old Testament: A Guide to the Pentateuch* (Downers Grove: IVP, 2003) for an introductory discussion.

4. For fuller discussions of scribal techniques and attitudes see Kenneth A. Kitchen, *On the Reliability of the Old Testament* (Grand Rapids: Eerdmans, 2003), 368–71; David M. Carr, *Writing on the Tablet of the Heart* (New York: OUP, 2005) especially 26–33; Karel van der Toorn, *Scribal Culture and the Making of the Hebrew Bible* (Cambridge: Harvard UP, 2007), esp. 11–68.

whole unit. By this means I hope to arrive at an emic definition of the genre of Gen 1–11, that is an understanding of the nature of the text as it was understood by the original, or more exactly, the implied author and readers of the text.

But we cannot be content with just an emic understanding. The title of this book *Genesis 1–11: History, Fiction or Neither?* invites the expectation of an etic interpretation, i.e., how a modern reader should view the text. Such a reading will be partly determined by that reader's presuppositions, which may range from skeptical atheism to naïve fundamentalism. By embracing orthodox Christian assumptions, I hope to recover an approach to the text that does it justice in its biblical and theological contexts as the opening chapter of Holy Scripture.

Genealogies

We begin our study of the minor elements that make up Gen 1–11 with a look at its genealogies.[5] The simplest is a three-generation genealogy of Adam to Enosh via Seth (4:25–26). This is a simple *linear* genealogy, just tracing a single line from Adam to Enosh. Just before it comes the genealogy of Cain (4:17–24). Cain's genealogy is linear to begin with, tracing the direct descent Adam— Cain— Enoch— Irad— Mehiyael—Methushael—Lamech; but at the next step it becomes *segmented* naming three sons of Lamech: Jabal, Jubal and Tubal-cain. This pattern of a linear genealogy becoming segmented is found in 5:1–32: the genealogy of Adam via Seth and Noah concludes with the three sons of Noah— Shem, Ham, and Japheth. The genealogy of Shem to Abram is likewise linear with a segmented conclusion, "When Terah had lived 70 years he fathered Abram, Nahor, and Haran" (11:26).[6] But the Table of Nations (Gen 10) is segmented from the beginning. Japheth had seven sons and two of them, Gomer and Javan, fathered another seven sons between them.

What is the function of genealogies in general and these in particular? And, how do they relate to the book of Genesis as a whole? By themselves linear genealogies serve to connect the generations: Adam

---

5. For fuller discussion see Robert R. Wilson, *Genealogy and History in the Biblical World* (New Haven: Yale UP, 1977).

6. Biblical citations are from ESV except where indicated.

begets a son in his image, which, as the text points out, is the image of God. The genealogy implies that his further descendants are also in the image of God, and of course two of them are specially favored: Enoch is translated to heaven because he walked with God, and later on Noah is the only one to escape the flood because he was righteous and blameless in his generation.

Segmented genealogies on the other hand serve to make claims to territory or skills. The Table of Nations in Gen 10 is an elaborate segmented genealogy that shows how the nations of the then-known world were seen to be all descended from the sons of Noah. The much shorter segmented genealogy in Gen 4:20–22 shows how three of Lamech's sons founded guilds of herdsmen, musicians, and metalworkers. These interests, Lowery argues, show that the primary purpose of genealogies is not to relate history but to provide a charter for landholding and expertise in various areas.[7] These conclusions are supported by studies of genealogies in other oral cultures as well as by ancient Near Eastern texts.

But there are features of the biblical genealogies that are unusual. In Gen 5 the seventh generation from Adam is Enoch, renowned for his walk with God and for his translation to heaven: "he was not, for God took him" (5:24). Similarly, the genealogy in Gen 4 involves six generations of linear descent and then with the seventh generation, i.e. Lamech's sons, it becomes segmented. This interest in sevens is underlined by reference to Cain's threat of sevenfold vengeance and of Lamech's seventy-sevenfold revenge (4:24). This interest in sevens is also obvious in the structure of Gen 1 (see below) and in many Old Testament rituals. These features demonstrate careful organization of the text with a didactic purpose, not mere historiography.

Another unusual feature of two of the genealogies, 5:1–32 and 11:10–26, is that they note the ages of patriarchs when they fathered their first child and when they died. This feature occurs only in the elect lines of Adam to Noah, and Shem to Abram. Both genealogies cover ten generations, which again looks like deliberate planning and not chance, whereas genealogies of the non-elect (e.g., Cain's genealogy in 4:20–22 and the sons of Noah in chapter 10) do not have this feature.

---

7. Lowery, *Towards a Poetics*, 81.

However, the number of nations or sons of Noah does, on some counts,[8] come to seventy, which raises the suspicion of artifice. That this total may be significant is made more likely by the groups of seven in the genealogy of Japheth who has seven sons and seven grandsons. Cush has five sons and two grandsons, and Egypt has seven sons (10:2–7, 13–14). These groups of seven underscore the significance of the total.

Whatever significance may be read out of this fondness for sevens, tens, and seventy, one conclusion is clear—these genealogies constitute the backbone of Genesis. This is particularly obvious in chapters 1–11, where narrative and genealogy alternate and the two main genealogies of Adam to Noah and Shem to Abram link the first human to Abram, the forefather of Israel. But this pattern of genealogy alternating with narrative continues in subsequent chapters. Each main section begins, "These are the generations of …:" Terah in 11:27–25:11 (=biography of Abraham); Ishmael in 25:12–18; Isaac in 25:19–35:29 (=biography of Jacob part 1); Esau in 36:1–37: 1; and Jacob in 37:2–50:26 (=biography of Jacob part 2). There are, in fact, ten[9] headings, "These are the generations of …." It should be noted how the terse genealogies in chapters 12–50 tell of the descendants of Abraham outside the elect line, i.e., Ishmael and Esau, while the long narratives of Abraham, Isaac, and Jacob tell the story of the chosen ancestors of Israel. The same is true, much more briefly, in the opening chapters. It is from Adam and Eve that all humans come, including the chosen line (2:4–4:26). Following this is a major genealogy (5:1–32), which concludes with Noah and his sons. The flood wipes out the non-elect leaving only the righteous and blameless Noah to survive (6:9–9:29).

Examining these genealogies and associated material closely, we can see that the genealogy in chapter 5 has been expanded by a comment that connects it with the narratives of chapters 2–4 and 6–9. Lamech, the father of Noah, prays at his son's birth: "Out of the ground that the Lord has cursed, this one shall bring us relief from our work and from the painful toil of our hands" (5:29). This is an obvious reference to the curse in 3:17, "Cursed is the ground because of you; in pain you shall eat

8. The remark about the Philistines in 10:14 looks like an aside, not an intrinsic part of the genealogy. Further discussion in Wenham, *Genesis 1–15*, 213–4.

9. Excluding 36:9 which seems to duplicate 36:1.

from it all the days of your life." Lamech hopes that his son will reverse the curse of his ancestor Adam. The terminology also looks forward to the flood story: "bring us relief" is the same root as "sorry" (6:6, 7); and "painful toil" comes from the same root as "grieve" (6:6).

The genealogy in chapter 5 ends half-way through the usual formula: "After Noah was 500 years old, he became the father of Shem, Ham and Japheth" (5:32). Had it followed the usual formula (cf. 5:25–27) this verse ought to have read: "When Noah had lived 500 years, he fathered Shem, Ham and Japheth. Noah lived after he fathered Shem, Ham and Japheth 450 years and had other sons and daughters. Thus all the days of Noah were 950 years." If one reads on in Genesis, one finds some of the missing elements of the full formula, "After the flood Noah lived 350 years. All the days of Noah were 950 years, and he died" (9:28–29). The formula has also been slightly modified to take account of the flood story, which has apparently been inserted between 5:32 and 9:28. This disruption of the genealogical formula is also found in the patriarchal narratives (cf. 11:26, 32; 21:5; 25:7, 19–20; 35:28–29; 37:2; 50:22–26).

Scholars are divided as to whether the genealogies or the narratives are the earlier elements in Genesis. Though most believe that the narratives came first and the genealogies were added later, I think there are good reasons for maintaining the opposite and seeing the narratives as expanding the genealogies.[10] This sequencing of the material is hard to prove, but looking at the present final form of Gen 1–11, one must agree that the narratives do elaborate on people in the genealogies. Thus as a first approximation one could describe the genre of Gen 1–11 as an expanded genealogy.

Genesis 1:1 – 2:3

Such a definition of the genre fits Gen 2:4–11:32. But the opening chapter (more precisely 1:1–2:3) falls outside these limits. This chapter prefaces the main body of Gen 1–11, each section of which is headed by the formula, "These are the generations of ...." The first of these headings occurs in 2:4, "These are the generations of the heavens and the earth" and introduces the narratives about Adam, Eve, and Cain. Often, 2:4 is

10. Wenham, Genesis 1–15, 121–3 and Wenham, "The Priority of P," Vetus Testamentum 49 (1999): 240–58.

supposed to conclude the opening chapter, but this is a mistake.[11] Everywhere else in Genesis it is a heading introducing what follows, not summarizing what precedes, and there is no reason to take 2:4 as summary rather than heading. We should therefore read 1:1–2:3 as a prelude or overture to the main body of Gen 1–11, if not to the whole Pentateuch.

Chapter 1 is a carefully constructed unit in its own right, which equips the reader with the theological spectacles that enables him to read the subsequent material with the correct focus. There are various marks of careful editing that characterize chapter 1. There is chiastic linkage between the opening verse (1:1) and the closing verses (2:1–3). Verse 1 literally reads "In the beginning *created* (A), *God* (B), *heavens and earth* (C)" and these terms reappear in reverse order in 2:1–3. Not only is there chiastic linkage but both 1:1–2 and 2:1–3 are multiples of seven words: 1:1 consists of seven words, 1:2 of fourteen (7 x 2), and 2:1–3 of thirty-five (7 x 5) words. Other key terms in 1:1–2:3 are also multiples of seven: God occurs thirty-five times, earth twenty-one times, and the clauses "and it was so" and "God saw that it was good" also occur seven times. This preference for multiples of seven draws attention to the seventh day, the Sabbath, the day when God rested from his acts of creation. Seven is of course a sacred number throughout the Old Testament. Many ritual gestures are repeated seven times. It is not only the seventh day of the week that is holy, but the seventh month, the seventh year, and the jubilee year, which occurs every fifty years (50 = 7 x 7 + 1).

Other marks of careful arrangement are visible in the six days of creative activity. Eight works of creation take place in six days. This is achieved by having twice as many works on days three and six as on other days. What is more, if the creation week is split in half, the works of the second half of the week correspond to those in the first half. Thus, on day one God creates light, on day four the greater and lesser lights; on day two the sky and sea, and on day five the birds and fish; and on day three the land and plants, and finally on day six animals and man. Day seven stands apart to mark the unique status of the Sabbath.

This careful structuring of this first account of creation sets it apart from the material that follows in the subsequent chapters. So does the language. Whereas 2:4 onwards is straightforward Hebrew narrative

---

11. Wenham, *Genesis 1–15*, 49–56.

prose, 1:1–2:3 has a poetic flavor, and though some scholars have termed it poetry it is better described as elevated prose. It certainly has a different character from the later chapters of Genesis.

But can one be more specific about its genre? Hermann Gunkel called it "faded myth" while Von Rad said it was not myth or saga but priestly doctrine.[12] There is some merit in both these descriptions, but better than both is Westermann's description of this section as an overture.[13] An overture opens an opera and introduces some of the key themes and tunes that will be developed later: this is what Gen 1 does for the rest of the book. In Gen 1 we meet for the first time some of the chief actors and learn something about their character.

The God of Genesis is quite different from the traditional gods of the ancient Near East.[14] In Gen 1 only one God is active; there are no other gods and goddesses such as are found in other ancient cosmologies. Not only is this one God unique, he is also omnipotent. With just a few words of command and no apparent struggle, the entire world is called into being; even the sun, moon, and stars, which are deities in other cultures, are created by the divine word. Besides presiding omnipotently over his creation, the God of Genesis creates with a purpose. He creates an environment where mankind can flourish. The creation of those elements most needful for human development—such as dry land, plants and fruit trees, the heavenly bodies—is described more fully than other aspects. But God's particular concern for man is demonstrated by assigning him the plants for food. Other ancient cultures say mankind was created to provide the gods with food. Genesis says the opposite: God provides man with food. Another mark of divine benevolence towards man is his Sabbath rest. The creation of man is the climax of Gen 1. Both male and female are created in God's image, which means they are to be his representatives on earth. And another implication of man's divine image is that he should imitate God by observing the Sabbath.

---

12. Hermann Gunkel, *Genesis* (9th ed.; Göttingen: Vandenhoeck & Ruprecht, 1977), xiv and Gerhard von Rad, *Genesis: A Commentary* (2nd ed.; London: SCM, 1972), 47, respectively.

13. Westermann, *Genesis*, 93. According to Westermann Genesis 1 is a festive overture to P, a putative source of the Pentateuch supposedly responsible for the genealogies among other texts.

14. On the nature of biblical monotheism see Michael S. Heiser, "Monotheism and the Language of Divine Plurality in the Bible and the Dead Sea Scrolls," *Tyndale Bulletin* 65 (2014): 85–100.

God's rest on the Sabbath implies something else. In the ancient world the dedication of a temple took a week and on the seventh day the god or gods came to take up residence in it. It seems likely that the creation of the world is viewed as creating a temple for the Creator who rests on the seventh day, i.e., comes to dwell on earth, his newly created temple.[15] In other words, the goal of creation is that God should "rest," i.e., dwell with man. All students of Scripture will recognize theological motifs in Gen 1 that are developed more fully later in Genesis, indeed in the rest of the Bible. The one theme that is missing from Gen 1 is the effect of sin on human life and particularly on the God-man relationship. But Gen 3 onwards says plenty about the growth of wickedness and the dire effects of sin on all aspects of human life. Despite this absentee from the opening chapter, Gen 1 is a brilliant overture to Genesis as a whole. Its ideas are foundational and well-developed in later material.

This analysis of Gen 1 shows it to be an elaborate literary construct that makes it a worthy gateway into Genesis. More than that, it introduces key theological principles that inform book after book of the Bible. It defines the God of Israel by contrasting his character and power with the multitude of weak and petulant deities that inhabited the thought world of surrounding societies. If one sees the genealogies as forming the backbone of Genesis, one could call Genesis 1 its head, in that its leading ideas flow out from it. However, this is not to say that Gen 1 is the same genre as the genealogies. We observed that, unlike later chapters, Gen 1 is not headed by the title "These are the generations of," which distinguishes Gen 2:4 onwards from what precedes it. Gen 1 is therefore an independent introduction to the rest of Genesis. It could stand by itself, but in its present setting it orients the reader to what follows by elucidating the presuppositions that inform the subsequent narratives.

Narratives in Genesis 2:4 - 11:9

It is these narratives from the garden of Eden to the Tower of Babel that dominate Gen 1–11 and essentially define its character. We have seen that these narratives serve, basically, to expand the genealogies that form the backbone of the opening chapters. This must be taken into account in establishing the genre of Gen 1–11.

---

15. See John H. Walton, *The Lost World of Genesis 1* (Downers Grove: IVP, 2009), 72–92.

But if we look at these stories one-by-one and temporarily disregard their present context, it is clear that they function to explain present experiences by relating the past. Thus chapter 2 relating the creation of Adam and Eve explains the necessity of marriage and the nature of the marriage union. Marriage is needed to prevent loneliness, "It is not good that the man should be alone" (2:18). It is also necessary if the human race is to survive and fulfill the creation mandate to "be fruitful and multiply" (1:28). Making Eve out of Adam's rib shows the nature of the bond between man and wife. Marriage connects the partners to each other as though they were blood relatives. They are each other's flesh and bone (cf. 29:14). They become like brother and sister to each other in the closeness and permanence of their relationship. And the universality, or at least paradigmatic quality, of Adam and Eve's experience is emphasized by the closing editorial comment on the story: "Therefore a man shall leave his father and mother and hold fast to his wife, and they shall become one flesh" (2:24).

Similarly chapter 3 offers a story that explains the nature of sin and its consequences. The essence of sin according to Gen 3 is disobeying God. He had given Adam and Eve just one rule, but they disregarded it by eating from the tree of knowledge. There were immediate consequences: ashamed, they hid among the trees. There were long-term consequences spelled out in the curses: hard work to keep themselves fed, danger from animals such as snakes, pain in childbirth, death, and exclusion from the garden where they could have eaten of the tree of life and lived forever. These features characterize to a greater or lesser extent every sinful deed, but by telling a story Genesis makes these points much more vividly than a generalizing theological abstraction. We could say that this story offers a paradigm of sin. This is confirmed by the next story in Genesis, the murder by Cain of his brother Abel. There are many parallels between chapters 3 and 4 which underline the point that both stories offer paradigmatic descriptions of sin.

Myth: An Inappropriate Category

Anthropologists and religious phenomenologists describe stories about the distant past, which explain present phenomena, as myths, especially where the divine is involved. And I have argued that this is what the opening chapters of Genesis do. They explain relationships between man and beast, between man and woman. They picture monogamous heterosexual marriage. They explain the presence of toil, pain, and death. And in describing these phenomena, they both prescribe a pattern for society—life in the garden of Eden gives a glimpse of the ideal—and they describe what the life of an ancient Israelite farmer was like—life outside the garden—enduring the curses of Gen 3. So there is no doubt that phenomenologists would be quite at ease describing Gen 1–11 as myth.

But calling Gen 1–11 myth is at least unwise, at worst misleading, and as I shall argue, inaccurate. Since the time of the ancient Greek philosophers in the fifth century BC, myths have had a bad press. Greeks contrasted the myths of Homer with the logic of the philosophers. Myths were regarded as irrational fiction as opposed to the truths of philosophy and history. Myths were an ornamental way of writing akin to poetry: reason and history used sober prose. This denigration of myth continued down the ages. Greek *mythos* was translated into Latin as *fabula*, from which English "fable" comes. Enlightenment thinkers from the eighteenth century also subscribed to the negative evaluation of myth and commonly viewed Gen 1–11 in this light. Many went even further and regarded all Scripture as myth, because it was written from a supernatural perspective, which modern secular thinkers thought was unacceptable. Thus, from de Wette to Bultmann, some Christian theologians have tried to demythologize the Bible. This involves removing the supernatural elements such as prophecy and miracles, extracting the historical core, and then retelling the material in a way that does not conflict with the biblical scholar's preferred philosophy.

While biblical scholars were applying these negative views of myth to the Scriptures, mythographers were developing a more positive understanding of myths. They are no longer seen as unscientific, unhistorical, and untrue. They are not irrational. Myths, on the contrary, represent a different way of expressing truth. They complement philosophy and history and express some of the fundamental ideas of the society that perpetuates them. They hold a mirror to that society, illuminating its nature, as well as portraying its ideas and worldview. They are particularly important for understanding social rituals.

Despite these modern attempts to enhance the standing of myth in scholarly perception, the word "myth" itself still has very negative overtones. According to one dictionary a myth is a "commonly held belief that is untrue or without foundation."[16] According to another, it is "a purely fictitious narrative usually involving supernatural persons."[17] The dictionaries also give more neutral definitions, but in everyday usage, "myth" usually characterizes a belief as false or misleading. And this is not how the first authors or hearers of these stories would have viewed them: they would doubtless have held them in similar respect to our era's respect for modern cosmologies or other scientific theories. For these reasons, it is prudent to avoid the term "myth" in describing the genre of Gen 1–11. As already mentioned, this has been the practice of the great twentieth-century commentators on Gen 1–11. Gunkel described it as "faded myth,"[18] von Rad preferred "priestly doctrine," while Westermann spoke of these narratives as *Urgeschichte*, "primeval history."

These terms do not exclude the possible historical reference of the narratives, but they also do not expressly affirm the historicity of any particular feature. There are, though, good reasons for affirming that the stories of Genesis are like history in some respects. For example, though Gen 3 offers a paradigm for every sin — disobedience, alienation, suffering — it is clear that some features of the narrative are unique and not repeated every time someone sins; Adam and Eve were naked when they ate the forbidden fruit but were clothed afterwards. Wearing clothes is taken by Genesis to be the usual current situation. Other permanent changes include living outside the garden, for subsequent sins (e.g. Cain and Abel) take place outside Eden. It is also likely that Genesis views toil, pain, and death as part of the human inheritance, not something that originates every time someone sins, even though every sin subsequent to Adam and Eve's confirms the justice of the divine punishments. On a more positive note, one can be sure that ancient Israelites did not think the creation of every woman involved the cloning of a man! Though the creation of Eve from Adam's rib was an illustration of general principles about marriage, and in this sense

---

16. *The Chambers Dictionary* (Edinburgh: Chambers, 2003).

17. *Shorter Oxford English Dictionary* (London: OUP, 1959).

18. That is, stories that were seen as myths in older cultures, but in Genesis expressed a different theology.

paradigmatic, there is also a uniqueness about their relationship that is not replicated universally. For this reason I think these chapters should also be seen as protohistorical. These chapters contain stories that both illustrate important social and theological principles, as myths are often alleged to do, yet they also tell of unique occurrences. These may not be datable and fixable chronologically, but they were viewed as real events.

This is confirmed by the way these narratives are attached to the genealogies. Genesis, as we have seen, traces the family tree of the sons of Jacob right back to Adam (see Gen 5, 11, and sundry genealogical notes from chapters 12 to 50). But this bare genealogical framework is interrupted and expanded at various points by narrative. The implication would seem to be that if the later figures in the genealogies are real people — and they certainly behave in very human fashion — then the earlier characters, the ancestors of Abraham, must also be viewed as real persons. The ages of the patriarchs at the birth of their first sons and at their death changes dramatically down the genealogies, ranging from 969 with Methuselah to 110 with Joseph. This may be a hint that in some way the earlier antediluvian patriarchs were viewed differently from the postdiluvian successors, but this is guesswork.

As an interim conclusion we may say that Gen 1–11 is a genealogy, which has been expanded with stories from ancient times to produce an account of the development of the human race from its origin to the time of Abraham. This account reflects ideas current in the ancient Near East in the first and second millennia BC, but in various ways decisively contradicts them. Polytheism and many of its associated beliefs (e.g., about mankind's role) are refuted by Gen 1–11. But there are texts from Mesopotamia that parallel Gen 1–11 that may be utilized in an attempt to clarify the genre of Gen 1–11.

Some Mesopotamian Parallels to Genesis 1–11

The best known of these texts is the Atrahasis epic (c. 1600 BC). It is a long poem written in Akkadian that begins with the god Ea creating seven human couples to take over the work of the lesser gods whose task was to till the land to grow food for the great gods. Tiring of the effort, the lesser gods went on strike, and human beings were made in order to circumvent the problem. However, soon a population explosion threatened, so the great gods adopted various measures to combat the growth of the human race, the last being a universal flood. From this disaster, one man, Atrahasis (=Noah), and his family were saved by building an ark in which they and the animals survived the flood. The flood is described more completely in tablet 11 of the Epic of Gilgamesh, another Mesopotamian text from about 1600 BC. However, the context of the flood story in Gilgamesh is quite different from the Atrahasis epic, which provides a much closer analogy to the setting of the flood story in Genesis.

While the Atrahasis epic offers good parallels to the narrative elements in Gen 1–11, it is the Sumerian King List (c. 1900 BC) that furnishes the better parallel to the genealogies. The Sumerian King List tells of eight, nine, or ten kings[19] whose reigns lasted up to 43,200 years each. It then mentions that a flood swept over the earth and kingship had again to be lowered from heaven. These postdiluvian kings reigned for fewer years than their pre-flood predecessors — just hundreds of years instead of millennia. This pattern of very-long-lived kings, followed by a flood, then long-lived kings is akin to the pattern in Gen 1–11, where very-long-lived patriarchs (Gen 5) are succeeded by a flood and then by long-lived patriarchs (Gen 11). This shows that the structure of Gen 1–11 has a long pedigree stretching back to the early second millennium BC.

There is yet another Sumerian text that matches the pattern of Gen 1–11 even more precisely by mixing genealogical elements and epic narrative even more intimately. This is the Sumerian Flood Story, renamed by Thorkild Jacobsen "The Eridu Genesis."[20] The tablets on which this epic is written are unfortunately broken and Jacobsen had to reconstruct it in some parts. It begins, apparently, with the creation of man and the animals. Then, it tells of one of the goddesses trying to improve man's lot by settling him in cities. This apparently failed. So, kingship was introduced, which enabled the building of cities and the institution of wor-

19. Different texts of the king list have different numbers of kings. One version is in James B. Pritchard, *Ancient Near Eastern Texts* (2nd ed.; Princeton: Princeton University Press, 1955): 265.

20. See Thorkild Jacobsen, "The Eridu Genesis," *Journal of Biblical Literature* 100 (1981): 513–29, reprinted in Richard S. Hess and David T. Tsumura, *I Studied Inscriptions from Before the Flood* (Winona Lake: Eisenbrauns, 1994), 129–42.

ship. A list of pre-flood kings followed and then the familiar flood story. Jacobsen notes that "to find this chronological list form ... combined with simple mythological narrative is truly unique. It suggests that the Eridu Genesis depends directly on the Kinglist and its style."[21] But that is only one of the features that makes the Eridu Genesis like the biblical one. Other significant parallels are: (1) beginning the account with creation, (2) listing long-lived leading figures from the past (kings/patriarchs), (3) the flood, (4) organizing the narrative quasi-historically in terms of cause and effect, and (5) the great interest in chronology (length of reigns/lives). Jacobsen comments that this interest in chronology makes it more like chronicles and historiography.[22] For this reason he characterizes both the Eridu Genesis and Gen 1–11 as mytho-historical, "We may assign both traditions to a new and separate genre as mytho-historical accounts."[23] This is a sensitive analysis of the nature of both texts, but as argued earlier "myth" is a loaded term, which, when applied to Scripture, leads to misunderstanding. A term is required that does not suggest to many readers that the account is make-believe, but one that affirms its truth and validity. This is why I prefer to describe Gen 1–11 as protohistory. It is proto in that it describes origins, what happened first. It is also proto in that it is setting out models of God and his dealings with the human race. It is historical in that it is describing past realities and the lessons that should be drawn from them.

If then we are seeking a definition of the genre of Gen 1–11, protohistory, I maintain, is the best we can do. It is not ordinary history that relies on contemporary sources, or at least on sources much closer to the events it describes than Gen 1–11 does. On the other hand it is not fiction, whose basis is in the author's imagination rather than stimuli from the external world. Yet, protohistory shares with both these genres the aim of imparting an interpretation of the world as we experience it. It could be described as theology and sociology in pictures. But whereas history could be described as a photograph of the past and fiction as a movie, protohistory is akin to a portrait of the past. It is a valid representation that faithfully portrays the artist's intentions. And it is these

---

21. Ibid., 141 = *JBL*, 528.
22. Ibid.
23. Ibid., 140 = *JBL*, 528.

intentions that the modern reader must focus on. He is not obliged to decide whether this detail or that is historical or imaginative interpretation. Hopefully our stance will be clarified by looking at three episodes in Gen 1–11.

The Sons of God and the Nephilim (6:1 - 4)

The plot of Gen 1–11 does not always run smoothly. The long genealogy of chapter 5 does not lead directly into the flood story but is interrupted by 6:1–4, which relates how the sons of God, or the sons of the gods, married women who then gave birth to the giant Nephilim. To the modern Western reader this seems the stuff of fantasy and many commentators find no difficulty in describing the episode as myth. If myth is defined as stories about the gods from ancient times, this certainly seems to fit that definition. And with its characterization as myth goes a tendency not to take it seriously, despite modern mythographers' insistence that fundamental beliefs about gods and societies are often expressed through myth. It seems wiser to explore how a different genre designation might allow a more positive approach to this passage. I shall therefore attempt to develop an emic understanding of this story and try to read it through the eyes of an ancient Israelite, not those of a secularized commentator.

The first item to note about this episode is its current context in Genesis. It parallels the Tower of Babel story, which explains the dispersion of peoples across the globe and the origin of language diversity. But the Babel story comes after the Table of Nations (chapter 10), which lists the nations of the ancient world known to Israel. Thus, chronologically the Babel story comes before the Table of Nations. Similarly, Gen 5 tells of the antediluvians being fruitful and multiplying by having "other sons and daughters." Evidently, the sons of God were active in the era covered by the genealogy. This episode is placed next to 6:5–8, the first announcement of the flood with its devastating assessment of human nature, "The LORD saw that the wickedness of man was great in the earth, and that every intention of the thoughts of his heart was only evil continually" (6:5).

This is the most severe assessment of the human heart and its propensity to sin in Genesis, if not in the whole Bible. And immediately following the sons of God episode, it seems to be a commentary on it. Clearly it is condemning the behavior of the sons of God and the daughters of man in no uncertain terms. But what exactly were they doing that merited such condemnation?

Three explanations[24] have had a strong following at different times. The first sees it as a condemnation of intermarriage between the good Sethite sons of God, the elect line, and the evil Cainite daughters of men, the non-elect line. This would foreshadow the later prohibition of Israelites marrying non-Jews and fits in with calling Israel "the son of God" occasionally. Though this has at times been a popular explanation among Christians, it seems rather forced to divide humanity this way. Were not the Cainites just as much sons of God as the Sethites? Or to put it the other way round, just as much daughters of man as the Cainites?

The second explanation is that the sons of God were kings who press-ganged girls into their harems, taking "as their wives any they chose." This view has had a strong following among Jewish interpreters. While the Israelite king is sometimes called God's son (e.g., Ps 2:7), there is no hint of compulsion or irregularity in the sons of God "seeing," "taking," and "choosing." All are legitimate actions within marriage proceedings. Nor is it clear why human kings should be called gods, yet human women be called daughters of men. Rather, the text seems to be contrasting the nature of the two parties.

This brings us to the third explanation: that the sons of God are spirits or angels. Ancient Israelites and their Near Eastern contemporaries would have viewed them as less important and powerful than the high God(s). These creatures are mentioned in various places in the Old Testament. They are members of the divine council who in Job 1:6 and 2:1 report back to the LORD on what is happening in the earthly realm. In the Psalms they are summoned to worship the LORD, 'Worship him all you gods (97:7; cf. 95:3; 97:9; 96:4). This understanding is found in Jewish writings of the pre-Christian era, in the New Testament (2 Peter 2:4; Jude 6, 7), and in the Early Church Fathers, that is, Christian writers of the first three centuries. Most modern commentators have therefore come to accept this interpretation of the phrase. It is pointed out

---

24. For fuller exposition of these views see Wenham, *Genesis 1–15*, 139–41.

that there was a widespread belief that great men of the past were god-man hybrids. Gilgamesh was reckoned to be one third divine and two thirds human. In the classical world, Zeus was held to have fathered Perseus, Heracles, and Alexander the Great, and Apollo is said to have fathered Plato, Pythagoras, and Augustus.[25] Genesis calls such hybrids the Nephilim, or "the mighty men who were of old."

But what makes this episode so heinous that a universal flood is called for? And what social practices are challenged by God's rejection of these "marriages"? The terminology of the episode is reminiscent of the fall. There, the woman *saw* that the tree was *good*, here the sons of God *see* the daughters were *good* (ESV "attractive;" 3:6; 6:2). There she *took*, here they *took*. There, God prevented Adam and Eve from eating of the tree of life so that they could not live forever. Here, God limits human life to 120 years (3:22; 6:3). These parallels make the sons of God emulate Eve in leading the other party into sin. Then, if we look at ancient marriage customs we may glimpse why not only the sons of God were to blame but also the human parties. Marriage in Bible times was essentially arranged by the males in the family, especially the father of the bride, who had to consent to the match. If there was no coercion involved and the proper form was followed, the girls' fathers were just as responsible for consenting to these unions as the sons of God in proposing them. This may be a clue to the social custom being pilloried. Not only did the ancients believe that some of their great heroes were the offspring of divine-human marriages, but such unions were encouraged by consigning girls to sanctuaries where a priest representing the deity could have intercourse with them.[26] Such sacred prostitution was believed to promote fertility in the fields and in other women. If this scenario is correct, Genesis is putting a very different spin on such activity: far from divine-human intercourse bringing fertility and long life, it prompted a universal flood. Certainly some abuse of sexual intercourse is being challenged, for a recurring theme in Genesis and later law is the abominable sexual practices of the Canaanites,

---

25. John Day, *From Creation to Babel: Studies in Genesis 1–11* (London: Bloomsbury Academic, 2013), 95.

26. On sacred prostitution in the ancient Near East see Richard S. Hess, *Israelite Religions: an Archaeological and Biblical Survey* (Grand Rapids: Baker Academic, 2007) 332–35; Edward Lipinski, "Cultic Prostitution in Ancient Israel?" *Biblical Archaeology Review* 40.1 (2014): 48–56, 70.

which are foreshadowed in Ham (9:22–27), practiced in Sodom (19), and denounced in the law (Leviticus 18).

There is another aspect to this episode that makes it reprehensible and connects it to the fall narrative. We noted that God's sentence on mankind for this activity was to limit human life to 120 years and that this is reminiscent of his decision after the fall to expel mankind from the garden, "lest he reach out his hand ... and eat, and live forever" (3:22). In other words, the union of the sons of God with the daughters of man is the second of three episodes in Gen 1–11 where man attempts to trespass on the divine realm and is punished for it: the third episode is the Tower of Babel. In this case, the sentence of 120 years explains why the ages of the postdiluvian patriarchs in 11:10–26 gradually decline, eventually with Moses reaching 120 as a general maximum.

This makes another link between this story of marriages and the contemporary experience of its original authors and readers. It is not simply about "the mighty men who were of old" but about the Nephilim, who were still around when the Israelite spies visited Canaan (Numbers 13:33). And the practice of cultic prostitution was still current throughout the biblical period; it even survived to quite modern times in parts of the East. It is these connections with later historical practice that makes this account more than a myth. The characterization as proto-history captures both the lively social comment that it enshrines and the historical realities on which it is commenting. Within the book of Genesis it contributes to the picture of ever-increasing sinfulness and man being evermore daring in challenging God. This avalanche of sin now culminates in such universal violence that a flood is necessary to sweep away the old creation and start again with a new world order. To this, the longest episode in Gen 1–11, we now turn.

The Flood Story

The first item to note about the story of the flood in Genesis is that "The Flood Story" is not the biblical heading, which is, "These are the generations of Noah," or more precisely, "This is the family history of Noah" (6:9). Thus, the story does not end with the exit from the ark but with the curse on Canaan. The author of Genesis saw "The Family History of Noah" as 6:9 to 9:29. 6:5–8 is not part of the "Family

History"but a trailer for it, introducing some of the key points of the next section.[27] In trying to arrive at an emic definition of the genre, we must include the rules on eating, the talion law, attitudes to drunkenness and to the Canaanites. We should also recall that the flood story is the part of Genesis with the closest extra-biblical parallels in the Atrahasis and Gilgamesh epics.

We have already noted how the Atrahasis epic has a similar structure to Gen 2–9: it begins with the creation of mankind and ends with Noah (Atrahasis) offering sacrifice after the flood. But though the outlines of the plot are similar, the details are very different, springing out of quite distinct theologies. The monotheism of Genesis contrasts with the polytheism of Atrahasis. God's provision of food for man in Genesis conflicts with man producing food for the gods in Atrahasis. The flood is sent not because humanity is proliferating and disturbing the peace of the gods, but because of the corruption of the human heart and mankind's addiction to violence. According to the Babylonian tradition, once the flood was unleashed it was out of the gods' control, but the LORD only has to remember Noah for the flood to decline (8:1). After the flood the Babylonian god Enki decrees that childbirth and infancy should be made more difficult to limit population growth, whereas Genesis repeats three times the first command given to man: "Be fruitful and multiply"; Genesis then adds material without parallel in Atrahasis. To instill respect for all life, meat may only be eaten if the lifeblood is thoroughly drained out. To prevent the violent like Lamech (4:24) from overrunning the earth again and provoking another flood, Genesis institutes strictly proportional retribution "whoever sheds the blood of man, by man shall his blood be shed" (9:6). Not only is violence still a potential problem, but there is the incorrigible human heart (6:5; cf. 8:20–22). Will that not trigger another flood? Not if sacrifice is offered by a righteous man such as Noah, declares 8:22. Yet, even the righteous may trip as Noah does drinking too much wine, which, in turn, provokes his son to act in a most unfilial manner.[28]

---

27. On the use of trailers in Genesis see Wenham, *Genesis 1–15*, 97.

28. For attempts to specify Ham's sin see the commentaries. I now think the most plausible explanation is that Ham was guilty of homosexual incestuous rape or at least homosexual incestuous lust. See Robert A. J. Gagnon, *The Bible and Homosexual Practice* (Nashville: Abingdon, 2001), 63–71.

In these ways, Genesis takes the traditional ancient Near Eastern account of the flood and by retelling it, presents a fresh and challenging vision of God and man. We meet a God who is almighty yet cares for man's needs, but also a God who hates and punishes sin, even though it is intrinsic to the human condition and leads, if unchecked, to unbridled violence. These tendencies are curbed by dietary restrictions, limiting consumption to blood-free meat and to plants, and by instituting the talion principle of a life for a life in cases of murder. With these safeguards in place, Gen 9:11 affirms "Never again will all flesh be cut off by the waters of the flood."

Through these modifications to the traditional flood stories Genesis is justifying and safeguarding key principles of ancient Israel's life. The Genesis flood story explains why Israelites are ideally vegetarian and eat only blood-free meat. It explains why violence is so horrific and must be deterred by the death penalty. It explains why sacrifice is so important and saves the world from being extinguished by divine wrath. It inculcates caution in drinking wine, underlines the importance of filial loyalty, and warns of the danger posed by the Canaanites and their customs.

All these points are made whether we view the flood story as myth, history, or fiction. Current beliefs and practices of ancient Israel are being explained and justified. So, can we just leave the genre of the flood story undecided? It does have some features that make me think protohistory is a better description than myth or fiction, for it does more than explain current custom. It claims to be rooted in time, as the extraordinarily detailed dating of all the main phases of the flood shows. It began on the seventeenth day of the second month in Noah's 600th year. A year and ten days later the water had dried up and Noah was told to leave the ark (7:11; 8:14). Many stages in between are timed. This is clearly an affirmation of the story's roots in history. Another is the way the story is connected to the genealogy of chapter 5, as we have already seen. Finally, as Jacobsen pointed out, the interest in cause and effect as well as chronology within Eridu Genesis warrants that text being classed as mytho-historical. Gen 6–9 obviously has similar features, but for reasons already stated I think protohistorical is a better description of its genre than mytho-historical.

The Tower of Babel (11:1–9)

The Tower of Babel story is the second of three tales in Genesis of universal judgment: the first is the flood story (chs 6–9), and the third the destruction of Sodom and the other cities of the plain (chs 18–19). Gen 2–11 describes two declensions into sin. The first starts with the fall and culminates with the earth being filled with violence (6:11). The second begins with Noah's fall from grace consuming too much wine, is exacerbated by Ham's behavior, and climaxes in an attempt to enter the divine realm by building "a city, and a tower with its top in the heavens" (11:4). As before (3:22–24), God curbs human ambition by stepping in to frustrate their plans. The message of this tale is clear, but does it clarify the genre of Gen 1–11?

The message emerges whether we regard the Tower of Babel story as history, myth, fiction, or protohistory. There are, though, some features of this tale that make the last option the best description. It is clearly set in the distant past, sometime before the dispersal of the nations and the development of different languages that the Table of Nations described in chapter 10. It not only antedates the dispersal of the nations, it gives an explanation of this dispersal: it is to thwart human aspirations of acquiring divine powers. Though set in the remote past, it not only explains current realities, the existence of different nations and languages, but also the name of Babylon and its uncompleted ziggurat. According to *Enuma Elish* (often called the Epic of Creation), a Mesopotamian story that celebrates Marduk's supremacy over the divine pantheon, the temple in Babylon called Esagila, which means "house whose top is high," had its top in heaven and its foundation in the underworld.[29] Genesis is clearly mocking this notion. Far from the tower reaching heaven, God had to come down to see it. Another claim of Babylon, that it was the religious capital of the known world, is sent up by the etymology of Babel offered by Genesis. In Akkadian *bāb-il(im)* means "Gate of God," evidently suggesting that at Babylon, man could get near to the gods. But Genesis connects Babel to the verb *bālal* "to confuse." God says, "Let us confuse (*nābēlāh*) their language." In other words, Babylon's name recalls God's judgment on human pride when he dis-

---

29. A. R. George, *House Most High: The Temples of Ancient Mesopotamia* (Winona Lake, IN: Eisenbrauns, 1993), 139 §967.

persed the nations and prevented them communicating with each other by making them speak different languages. Further derision of Babylonian pretensions is suggested by another word that sounds similar to *nābēlāh*: *nēbālāh* means "folly." So, one should not speak of the Tower of Babel but of the "Folly of Babel."

This animosity towards Babylon's claims is a recurrent theme in the Old Testament and could have arisen at various times, but the failure to complete the tower suggests a period in which the ziggurat of Babylon was at least in disrepair. A possible setting is the reign of Nebuchadnezzar 1 (1123–1101 BC) whose failure to complete his great construction projects became an occasion for jest and legend. Be that as it may, the story of the Tower of Babel evidently connects it with later historical realities, even though it is set in the distant past. So once again, I would suggest protohistory comes closer to characterizing the original genre of the passage than other suggested alternatives.

Conclusion

In this essay I have argued that recovering the message of Gen 1–11 is more important than defining its genre. A secure definition of its genre would clarify the interpretation of this text somewhat, but not fundamentally alter our understanding of it. I have advanced reasons for holding that protohistory is a better category for its genre than other proposed alternatives. I argued that the backbone of Gen 1–11 is an expanded linear genealogy: ten generations from Adam to Noah and ten generations from Noah to Abram. Most figures in these genealogies are simply known by their names and their age when they fathered their first-born and their age at death. But a few of them have extra details attached to them such as Lamech's prayer for his son Noah or the observation that Enoch walked with God. At other times the additional comments balloon into long accounts about the garden of Eden or the flood, but this does not obscure the point that these stories are add-ons to the chronological backbone of the genealogy. This interest in chronology and the causal explanation of the sequence of events in the dim and distant past makes protohistory a better description of Gen 1–11 than myth on the one hand and history on the other.

This conclusion is compatible with our analysis of three of the episodes attached to the genealogy. The angel marriages story reads at first like myth, in that it deals with divine activity in a way that modern readers usually regard as fantasy. But, I argued that for the ancient reader this was not the case. They believed certain great historical figures were indeed human/divine hybrids and that cult prostitution acted out such unions in real life. The flood and the reduction of the human life span to a maximum of 120 years demonstrated to biblical man that this was not just imaginative fiction or myth.

Similarly, the flood story is primarily a didactic narrative showing the seriousness of sin, especially cult prostitution and violence. It also explains the origin of the rules on meat eating, promotes the procreation of children, and introduces the law of talion to prevent unlimited revenge and an explosion of violence. The Genesis flood story retells a familiar ancient Near Eastern tale to teach a new theology and ethic. Genesis shows that there is only one supreme God whose all-powerful control of events warrants the description almighty. And whereas most ancient Near Eastern deities were rather lax in their morals, the God of the Genesis flood is supremely interested in good behavior. These ancient versions of the flood story have been termed mytho-historical because of their interest in causality and chronology. These features are even more prominent in Genesis, but to avoid the misleading associations of myth, I have called the accounts protohistorical.

The third episode we examined was the Tower of Babel. At one level it is mocking the religious pretensions of Babylon. Far from its top reaching heaven, it was so low that God had to leave heaven and descend to earth to see it. Babylon may pretend to be the gateway to heaven, but really, Babel spells confusion and folly. At one level the story is political satire, presumably with some contemporary features in view. But at a deeper level this is yet another attempt by humans to arrogate to themselves divine prerogatives. Adam and Eve, comprising the whole human race at that time, ate of the tree of knowledge and were expelled from Eden. Other humans practiced cult prostitution and violence and were swept away in the flood. If we regard these two stories as protohistorical, it follows that the Tower of Babel should also be classified as protohistorical. But there are hints within the story itself which point in the same direction. It is set in the distant past before languages and peoples diverged. Yet, it also relates to much later realities, showing knowledge of Babylon's claims and its building techniques using bricks and bitumen instead of stone and mortar. And, it looks forward to the story of Abraham to whom God promised to make a name, whereas he had frustrated the Babylonians' attempt to make a name for themselves. In this way there is linkage between the remote past and present reality, a typical feature of protohistory.

JAMES K. HOFFMEIER

Gordon Wenham has for decades produced solid scholarly work on the Pentateuch in general and the book of Genesis in particular. His two volume Word Biblical Commentary on Genesis is a magisterial work that remains an authoritative study even though it is more than twenty-five years old. His contribution to the present volume stands on the outstanding work he has already done.

I appreciate the approach he takes to Gen 1–11 here. He rightly seeks to distinguish between the authorial intent (the emic) and the expectations of the modern reader (the etic), and he seeks to bridge these reading strategies by approaching the biblical narratives by "embracing orthodox Christian assumptions." While he does not explain what is meant by these assumptions, I am inclined to think that the almost two millennia long tradition as regarding the stories of Gen 1–11 as reflecting real events may be in mind, but it might be helpful to know exactly what he means by "orthodox Christian assumptions."

I concur with his understanding of the function of the genealogies in Genesis. He sees them as the "backbone of Genesis" and Gen 1 as "its head, in that its leading ideas flow out from it." He recognizes that the Gen 1–11 genealogies are segments and symbolic numbers like seven and ten occur, and that the narratives are possibly expansions on the earlier genealogies. This observation, though contrary to prevailing opinion, seems reasonable to me. Wenham then suggests that "one could describe the genre of Gen 1–11 as an expanded genealogy." This proposal is nearly identical to what I have proposed in my chapter.

Wenham and I agree that it is "inappropriate" to classify Gen 1–11 as myth. My approach focused on the geographical realia of the Genesis narratives (especially the location of Eden). His rationale is that myth has negative connotations because Enlightenment minded scholars applied the category derived from Greek and Roman understanding of myth/fable to Scripture, leading to the demythologizing and the removal of the supernatural. Now as various scholars produce alternative definitions of myth that are less hostile towards religious faith, there remains too much confusion about myth and its negative connotation and it is thus prudent in Wenham's words "to avoid the term 'myth' in describing the genre of Gen 1–11."

Wenham rightly recognizes that because "the stories of Genesis are like history in some respects," a more appropriate genre needs to be sought. I resonate with his proposal of classifying Gen 1–11 as "protohistory" even if the events cannot be fixed chronologically, but nevertheless "were viewed as real events." He further clarifies that protohistory "is historical in that it is describing past realities and the lessons that should be drawn from them." I completely agree that Gen 1–11 deals with real people and events that serve as the basis for theological truth. It seems inconceivable that ancient Israelites religion, Judaism, and Christianity could establish their foundational doctrines about God and humanity based on pagan myths and concocted stories. In my paper here and in my response to Sparks, I argued that different types of history can be written, using various genres, and they were capable of reporting on real events that may not pass the authenticity test of modern critical analysis.

Wenham is careful to distinguish history, likening it to a picture or snapshot, from protohistory, which is more like an artist's painted portrait that, according to Wenham, "is a valid representation that faithfully portrays the artist's intentions." Distinguishing between a digital image and a painted picture is a helpful one that was advanced twenty years ago by V. Philips Long in his useful book, *The Art of Biblical History*. Long's and Wenham's idea about the distinction between the two modes of illustration is an insightful way to think about Genesis and what might be the expectations of the modern historian.

Wenham's treatment of the specific narratives covered in this volume is carefully reasoned and his consideration of ANE literary parallels is sound. I appreciate the fact that rather than simply looking at the similarities between the Gen 1–11 stories and Mesopotamian myths, he scrutinizes the differences. When doing such comparative literary analysis, differences are often more significant than parallels. Simplistic comparisons mean little and certainly do not constitute grounds for borrowing stories and reshaping them.

RESPONSE TO GORDON J. WENHAM

KENTON L. SPARKS

Dr. Wenham thoughtfully engages the literary details of Gen 1–11. He's been a close reader of Genesis for many years, having written a fine, two-volume commentary on the book, so I am not surprised in the least by his meticulous analysis of the text.[30] I agree with some of his points and disagree with others, but our exegetical differences are matters of personal judgment rather than bald fact. So, for example, while I agree with Wenham's insight about the literary and thematic links between the fall (Gen 3), the Nephilim (Gen 6), and the tower of Babel (Gen 11) episodes, I disagree with his fairly harsh judgment on Noah's drunkenness (Gen 9), which I regard as an innocent blunder rather than culpable fault. But again, these are matters of judgment. While I will be critical at many points in my response below, I want to say, from the outset, that I appreciate many elements in Wenham's essay. He is a thoughtful reader of Scripture.

Wenham's two volume commentary is far better than his essay. Despite some exegetical success, I don't find the essay all that helpful when it comes to our chief concerns: the genre and historicity of Genesis. Wenham seems to regard an understanding of the genres of Genesis, and of the book's historicity, as unnecessary luxuries. As I see it, this is because Wenham has not given sufficient attention to the generic theory that informs his discussion and, for this reason, has not understood the implications of genre for his reading of Genesis. The genre of Genesis has profound implications for its historicity, and its historicity has profound implications for how we read and engage the text theologically.

Now Wenham is far more open than Hoffmeier to the possibility that Gen 1–11 does not offer straightforward history, but he is no clearer in delineating what elements in the text do and do not pass as

---

30. Gordon J. Wenham, *Genesis* (2 vols.; WBC; Waco, TX: Thomas Nelson, 1987–1994).

historical representation. I'm not sure whether Wenham regards any portions of Gen 1–11 as straightforward history, much less whether and where Genesis gets the history right. Some of this confusion stems from Wenham's conflation of "representation" in general with "historical representation" proper. When Christians in the pew wonder about the historicity of Genesis, they are not asking whether, in some way, the text represents reality. They are asking whether the world was created in six literal days, whether humanity originated specially (without evolution), whether walking serpents once spoke, and whether Noah once built a giant boat. Wenham generally dodges these kinds of questions.

As I did in my response to Dr. Hoffmeier, I will engage Wenham's essay by distilling and responding to the various theses that he develops in his argument. I hope that my discussion fairly represents his perspectives and apologize in advance for any misunderstandings.

Wenham Thesis 1: The question to be considered is whether the early chapters of Genesis are history, myth, fiction, or "sui generis," a genre not attested elsewhere. But ultimately, the genre of Genesis is a secondary issue. Our primary concern must be the interpretation and application of the biblical stories.

Wenham's construal of our generic task in Gen 1–11 strikes me as theoretically thin and theologically reductionistic. With respect to theory, all intelligible discourse *must* conform to a significant degree with existing modes and patterns of discourse, else readers could not understand it. So whatever Genesis is generically, it cannot be *sui generis* (its own genre) in a restrictive sense. Gen 1–11 must be similar to and participate within the generic conventions of the ancient world. The only question is whether we can identify any similar texts that help us read Genesis well. For apart from these comparative exemplars, we will read Genesis as if it were written to suit our modern or private generic tastes, with all of the associated distortions in meaning and significance. But with this said, we can safely affirm from the outset that Genesis is, like all texts, *sui generis* in a sense, for it exhibits many unique traits not found in its generic siblings. So our generic work, properly construed, must attend to both similarities and alterities. One deficit in Wenham's essay is that he focuses almost exclusively on the *sui generis* alterities of Genesis and generally neglects the very important similarities between Genesis and other ancient texts.

Also problematic is Wenham's claim that he can successfully interpret and apply the biblical text without rendering generic judgment and, more specifically, without answering historical questions. As I see it, all interpretations imply an understanding of genre because one cannot "understand" a text if one has not decided what sort of text it is. Genre and understanding are sides of one coin. So Wenham is making generic judgments from beginning to end, whether he realizes it or not. The theoretical muddiness of Wenham's approach to Genesis is reflected in his indifference to the historicity of the text. He misunderstands the profound implications of historicity, or lack thereof, for interpreting and appropriating Genesis theologically.

Wenham Thesis 2: Whether one calls Gen 1–11 doctrine, history, fiction, or myth, the essential message of these chapters is clear.

Wenham seems to regard the historicity of the text as a minor generic problem, but the theological consequences of historicity are far from innocuous. To the extent that we judge the text as accurate history, to that same extent we must accept all narrated within the text as theologically binding. Let me explain.

When a narrative is not strictly historical, as in the case of an allegory or parable, the author does not intend every element in the story as binding on the reader. He might (for instance) intend the serpent in Genesis as a *symbol* of temptation's origins rather than as a literal creature that once walked upright and, having erred, was sentenced to life as a mute and slithering snake. But if the narrative is strictly historical, then the author intends us to embrace the whole of it—talking snakes and all. My point is that, in spite of Wenham's claim to the contrary, the "essential message" of the text is by no means clear irrespective of genre. Genre is the key to textual meaning and significance. And as I see it, some parts of Genesis, when regarded as historical, create grave theological, ethical, and scientific problems for modern, Christian readers. The historicity of Genesis is a subject that deserves more care than Wenham gives to it.

Wenham Thesis 3: Whatever label we use for Genesis, one generic label that does not suit Genesis is "myth." Myth is a poor designation for Gen 1–11 because, in common parlance, the word implies that the text is false and unreliable. Such an impression should be avoided because Genesis is God's word and, as such, is authoritative, reliable, and true.

Wenham at first claims that "myth" is an "inaccurate" label for Genesis, but his actual discussion supports only the more modest claim that this label can be misleading. I suspect that his drift from an absolute to softer resistance to myth parallels a subtle shift in his thinking, for he seems to move from an initial position in generic realism (which holds that myth, rightly defined, does not suit Genesis) to generic nominalism (which recognizes that the meaning of "myth" is a matter of convention and not hard fact).[31] At any rate, in the end I think that Wenham rejects "myth" as a matter of pastoral concern rather than generic substance. Although he seems to know that myths can represent reality as well as any other genre, he feels that, on balance, the word simply means "false" to the average person. So Christians should avoid describing any parts of the Bible as "myth." That is his logic.

While I share Wenham's pastoral concern and would not use "myth" in a Sunday morning sermon on Genesis, the present volume is a scholarly discussion for Christians who are asking sober questions about the historicity of Genesis. And for these Christians, the historicity of the text is far more pressing than the label we use to describe it. "Was there actually a world-wide flood and a giant boat?" "Did snakes once walk upright and speak human languages?" "Did God create the cosmos in six literal days?" These are their questions. And it is important that we admit candidly that these things simply cannot be historically right in the straightforward sense. Wenham seems willing to admit this but never says it with verve. I'd prefer that he come out of the proverbial closet. Little is gained by dodging the "m" word after he's divulged his pastoral motives for avoiding it. Myth, legend, fable, and tale are fine generic labels for some parts of Gen 1–11. Rather than avoid the word itself, let us argue instead that the myths of Genesis get at "the truth" better than other Near Eastern myths. Such a move allows the text to speak truly as God's word while divesting us of misplaced demands for historicity.

Wenham Thesis 4: If we wish to label Gen 1–11 generically, then "protohistory" is the best we can do. Protohistory is "neither fiction nor ordinary history." Rather, it represents "theology and sociology in literary pictures" and

---

31. For more on the difference between "generic realism" and "generic nominalism," see my essay in this volume.

"is akin to a portrait of the past." As such, readers are "not obliged" to decide whether this detail or that is historical or imaginative representation.

Wenham assigns to Gen 1–11 the generic label of "protohistory," a nebulous genre characterized (as near as I can tell) by its ambiguous stance on history. As Wenham sees it, the biblical author speaks of theology and sociology through "literary pictures" that stand between the generic extremes of "fiction" and "history." So the biblical author has not foisted upon us the onus of rendering historical decisions.

While I can certainly respect a candid admission that the text is historically ambiguous, in this case I question whether Wenham's conclusions are justified. First, in spite of his preference for historical ambiguity, Wenham's description of the narrative as a "literary picture" and denial that it offers "ordinary history" fits very nicely with what most scholars would call "fiction." For as usually conceived, fiction includes any narrative genre that does not closely represent the actual events of history. Secondly, irrespective of Wenham's generic opinion, some elements in Genesis, such as the flood story, simply *cannot* be historical because these do not fit into what is publicly known of natural and human history. If Wenham realizes this (as I suspect), then I would guess that his essay is designed rhetorically to satisfy two different audiences, namely, those who know Genesis cannot be historical and those who believe it must be history. This is a difficult road to travel, no doubt, but one that he seems to prefer over my approach.

As an aside, and perhaps this is a bit fussy, but I am troubled by Wenham's description of "fiction" as grounded in "an author's imagination *rather than* stimuli from the external world."[32] It seems to me that a simple contrast between "imagination" and "external stimuli" is misguided because the author's imagination is *always* shaped by and reflects influences from the external world. Apart from these stimuli, an author would have nothing to say nor any way to say it. Equally troubling is the related problem of Wenham's implicit bias against human imagination, which he seems to regard as something impoverished and unsuitable for God's word. Was it not a stroke of genius to have Eve taken from Adam's side, or to make tasty fruit a proxy for temptation, or to distance God from evil by casting blame on a crafty serpent? Karl Barth was

---

32. Italics mine.

right, I think, when he said that the authors of Genesis were God's true witnesses "not in spite of the fact but as and because they give their imagination free rein."[33] As the literary critics (apparently approved by Hoffmeier) have suggested, creative imagination stands behind much that is intriguing and powerful in the Bible.[34]

Wenham Thesis 5: Gen 1–11 is difficult to classify generically because the text comprises so many literary types, including genealogies, king lists, poems, and narrative material. A fruitful label for the whole might be "expanded genealogy," for it seems that the biblical author has used genealogy as a structural scaffold and integrated into this many different kinds of texts and traditions.

Wenham understands well the basic content of Gen 1–11. These early chapters of the Bible fold a portfolio of smaller traditions into a larger genealogical structure. A primary theme of the whole is etiology, that is, an explanation of how things in our world have come to be what they are. Whence came the cosmos, humanity, animals, plants, water, rainbows, nations, languages, nomads, and music? What caused human evil? Why must humanity labor in a world marked by suffering? Genesis offers an answer for each of these questions.

Wenham applies two different generic labels to Gen 1–11. It is "expanded genealogy," and it is "protohistory." As Wenham sees it, the author of this material "depicts the past" but is fascinated also with questions of theology, etiology, and sociology. The author's portrait of bygone days offers a rich assortment of generic types, including genealogies (linear and segmented), poems, and various narrative traditions. Whatever we make of the narrative elements, Wenham tells us that these are better described as "literary pictures" than as straightforward history.

There is a problem here. While labels like "protohistory" and "expanded genealogy" are just fine in and of themselves, they are essentially "dead ends" if they apply only to Genesis and not to other, similar ancient texts. In any language, we come to know the meaning of a given word by how it is used in many different contexts. The same is true of genre. We will not understand Genesis well apart from those ancient

---

33. Karl Barth, *Church Dogmatics* (5 vols. in 14; Edinburgh: T&T Clark, 1957–77), 3.1:92.

34. Imagination and creativity are central themes in the work of Robert Alter, Adele Berlin, and Meir Sternberg.

comparative exemplars that make its generic strategies intelligible. Can we improve on Wenham's generic categories?

I would like to suggest at this point that the traits described above fit well into the generic category that I have used in my own essay, namely, "ancient historiography." Ancient historians exploited chronologically-ordered lists, either king-lists or genealogies, and expanded these with other traditions and anecdotes to create portraits of the past. When their subjects were cosmic origins and early human history (what we might etically call "pre-history"), it was inevitable that they depended on the stuff of myth and legend rather than accurate histories. Sometimes the historians turned myth-makers, filling in early gaps with creative composition. As such, we are wise to read these texts for what they are rather than seek what they cannot offer. Ancient historians were simply in the dark about the actual events of early natural and human history. But they understood well the social and historical situation of their own day and could offer theologically astute insights about that context and the human condition generally. Good insight does not depend on historical precision.

Wenham Thesis 6: Uncertainties about the much-contested composition of Genesis "have only a limited effect on interpretation and genre assignment."

Wenham believes that our generic assessment of Genesis is not affected much by whether the book was assembled by one or several editors. I don't see how this can be right. While it is certainly true that some elements in Genesis existed before the book was written and can be assessed (to an extent) apart from the rest of the book, the contribution of each element to the book can be assessed only in light of the whole. If we sense strong coherence in the book, we will tend to interpret Genesis as the tightly-knitted message of a single author. But if we find it less coherent, our approach to the book will take a different path. We will assume that the book's editors were more comfortable than many modern readers with historical and theological ambiguity and, perhaps, more interested in offering insights for the human journey than a final destination. Allow me to illustrate the difference.

Wenham claims that the curse on Ham's son, Canaan, which appears at the end of the flood story, was intended as a warning against the dangers of the Canaanites and their customs (Gen 9:20–27). As developed by the biblical author, this provided a rationale for Canaan's servitude under Israel and, ultimately, for the extermination of the Canaanites and other inhabitants in the land, such as the Hittites, Jebusites, Amorites, etc. (see Gen 10:15). Framed in this way, Wenham's Genesis stands in support of violence against the foreigners who lived in Canaan.

I see things differently. While I acknowledge that this is one voice in Genesis, another author in Genesis has taken up a different position on the issue. Rather than setting the stage for violent conquest, this second author portrays Abraham—the forefather of Israel—as a close friend of the Hittites. Abraham does not kill the Hittites and seize their land. He humbly bows before Ephron the Hittite and pays for a modest plot of land in Canaan (see Gen 23).[35] Scholars have long noted that this second author (usually called the "Priestly writer," or P) uses "Hittite" interchangeably with "Canaanite," so there is no question about his basic point.[36] Whereas one author of Genesis assumed that Canaanites were marked for destruction, the other stood against this. And it is this second voice, which loves the enemy, that should carry the day in our Christian theology.[37]

Much is lost, generically and theologically, when we read a text that offers many perspectives as if it offers only one. Genesis is not only ancient historiography. It is an anthology that brings together the theological and historical ideas of several ancient Hebrew writers.

Conclusions

What is the generic character of the early chapters of Genesis, and what implications does this have for the historicity of the events narrated therein? Wenham describes more clearly than Hoffmeier the various traits that he sees in Gen 1–11 and provides suitable "labels" to charac-

---

35. As Wenham has noted, "The outstanding characteristic of this account is the courtesy and deference each side shows in the negotiations." See Wenham, *Genesis*, 2.126.

36. For the Priestly writer's use of the term "Hittite," see John Skinner, *A Critical and Exegetical Commentary on Genesis* (2nd ed.; Edinburg: T&T Clark, 1930), 336; also Wenham, *Genesis*, 2.124–26.

37. I actually regard this story as an expansion of P by a later editor more interested than either J or P in protecting the interests of foreign people. To explore how this theological problem was worked out in the New Testament, see Kenton L. Sparks, "Gospel as Conquest: Mosaic Typology in Matthew 28:16–20," *CBQ* 68 (2006): 651–63.

terize the parts and whole. He is also more candid regarding questions of historicity, implying at numerous points that the author of Genesis did not intend to depict history in a straight-forward sense. In these respects, I much prefer Wenham's approach to Hoffmeier's. But there are difficulties.

It seems to me that Wenham has neglected the insights of generic theory and for this reason has written an essay with various weaknesses. He claims that Genesis can be read apart from genre identification, but any attempt to read the text already entails generic judgment. Wenham, in fact, renders generic verdicts on every page of his essay. So the question is whether he does this well. My sense is that he does not. For having begun with a claim that Genesis can be understood apart from genre, Wenham proceeds to read the text, and to render generic decisions, without engaging seriously the comparative exemplars that make Genesis more intelligible. True, he does discuss the content of a few ancient exemplars (Atrahasis, the Sumerian King List, and the Eridu Genesis), but nothing is taken from these to help us understand Genesis. He instead focuses on the fact that Genesis is different. It is not "myth," nor "fiction," nor "legend," nor "tale." According to Wenham, Genesis stands in the space between history and these non-historical genres. He calls this "proto-history." And in doing so, Wenham leaves his readers hanging on the very questions that they care about. What stories in Genesis did not happen as narrated, and how should we read and interpret those parts of the text?

Irrespective of the label we put on it, Genesis is *very much* like the ancient myths, legends, and tales. Its authors were trained in and wrote using standard Near Eastern literary conventions. So with respect to genre, whatever is true of the ancient texts is to an extent true of Genesis. Namely, we can be sure that the scribes who wrote Genesis, like their foreign counterparts, drew on ancient sources, of varied historical quality, and also inherited or composed pieces of imaginative fiction and historical speculation. However valuable their texts are as theological voices, the early chapters of Genesis do not narrate closely what actually happened in natural and human history. We will read Genesis far better if we understand it as a theological commentary on the world known to the scribes than as a description of factual history.

CHAPTER THREE

GENESIS 1 – 11 AS ANCIENT HISTORIOGRAPHY

KENTON L. SPARKS

> "It is a disgraceful and dangerous thing for an infidel to hear a
> Christian, presumably giving the meaning of Holy Scripture, talk-
> ing nonsense on these topics; and we should take all means to pre-
> vent such an embarrassing situation, in which people show up vast
> ignorance in a Christian and laugh it to scorn."
>
> Augustine, *The Literal Meaning of Genesis*

Because the gospel is for all people and not for the Church alone,
Augustine believed that Christian interpretations of Scripture should
be true to the facts of "public knowledge" as understood by the larger
world to which the Church speaks. Aquinas expressed the same sen-
timent eight centuries later, when he warned that Christians "should
adhere to a particular explanation [of Scripture] only in such measure as
to be ready to abandon it, if it be proved with certainty to be false; lest
Holy Scripture be exposed to the ridicule of unbelievers, and obstacles
be placed to their believing."[1] It is no accident that these admonitions
were uttered in the context of interpreting the book of Genesis. For in
the days of Augustine, and even more so in the days of Aquinas, ten-
sions between a literal reading of Genesis and the insights of science
were growing with each advance in our understanding of the cosmos.
As is well known, the Church's response was slow and awkward. In the
seventeenth century it banned the astronomical works of Galileo, only

---

1. Aquinas, *Summa Theologica*, 1, q. 68.

to reverse course a century later as the accumulating evidence caved in on what was formerly considered an unassailable dogma of Scripture, tradition, and common sense.

Time has only widened the breach between science and Genesis. From where we stand now, at the dawn of the twenty-first century, in a time when we've sequenced the Neanderthal genome and traced out in the DNA our shared genetic heritage with primates and other mammals, it is no longer possible for informed readers to interpret the book of Genesis as straightforward history. There was no Edenic garden, nor trees of life and knowledge, nor a serpent that spoke, nor a worldwide flood in which all living things, save those on a giant boat, were killed by God. Whatever the first chapters of Genesis offer, there is one thing that they certainly do not offer, namely, a literal account of events that actually happened prior to and during the early history of humanity. If Genesis is the word of God, as I and other Christians believe, then we must try to understand how God speaks through a narrative that is no longer the literal history that our Christian forebears often assumed it to be.

Although I find evolutionary biology very interesting, I have no strong interest in discussing the relationship between Genesis and science. I mention it at the outset only because this essay, and the volume in which it appears, is evidence that some Christians are still embroiled in a debate that is elsewhere finished. Among Christian fundamentalists in the United States, who form a substantial element within what is usually described as Protestant "evangelicalism," there remains a significant assemblage of trained biblical scholars who still believe that Genesis offers a scientifically and historically accurate account of what actually took place in the nascent cosmos and early human history. These scholars find support for this interpretation of Genesis in the work of fundamentalist scientists, who employ various strategies to debunk the so-called "assured results" of modern astronomy and evolutionary biology. While I realize that some or many readers of this essay will value deeply this brand of fundamentalism, I should say up front that I find its approach to Scripture, and to science, entirely unsatisfactory. There is ample evidence that the authors of Scripture were not modern historians or scientists, and equally compelling evidence that evolutionary biology provides the best explanation for life's origins, including human origins.[2] Given this assumption, my primary task in this essay is to propose an approach to Genesis that allows informed Christians, living in these early decades of the twenty-first century, to read Scripture responsibly. To do this well, we will have to understand, as best we can, the literary genres used by the ancient authors to speak for God.

Musings on Genre

Genre is a loan word from the French, which in turn came from the Latin (*genus*) and, before that, from the Greek (*genos*).[3] The term, which means "type" or "kind," is widely used with reference to human discourse. To inquire about the genre of verbal discourse, whether of a spoken utterance or written text, is to ask about the sort of discourse that it is. Utterances might be "commands," "questions," "poems," or "stories," just as texts might be "biographies," "histories," "letters," or "newspaper articles." When we identify verbal discourse using one of these labels, we imply that we know something (or believe that we know something) about how that type of discourse works and that we have the competence to understand it to some degree. If we have this skill as interpreters of literature, scholars would say that we have *generic* or *literary competence*.

"Genre" should not be construed merely in terms of literature or art. It is better understood as an *epistemic function* of human interpretation in which we make sense of things by comparing them with other things. We compare and contrast, note similarities and differences, and formulate categories in which things fit or do not fit. The generic process is usually a tacit, unconscious operation in which we attend closely to neither the procedure nor its result.[4] We see a piece of fruit, judge that it's a tasty apple such as we've seen before, and take a confident bite. Nary is a thought given to this process unless the taste surprises us — for good

---

2. For a good summary of the evidence through a confessional lens, see Karl W. Giberson and Francis S. Collins, *The Language of Science and Faith: Straight Answers to Genuine Questions* (Downers Grove, IL: InterVarsity Press, 2011). For an accredited theological assessment, see Cardinal Joseph Ratzinger, *In the Beginning: A Catholic Understanding of the Story of Creation and the Fall* (Grand Rapids: Eerdmans, 1990).

3. For an introduction with bibliography, see Kenton L. Sparks, "Genre Criticism," in *Methods for Exodus* (ed. T. B. Dozeman; Cambridge: Cambridge University Press, 2010), 55–94.

4. See Michael Polanyi, *The Tacit Dimension* (Gloucester, MA: Peter Smith, 1983).

or ill. But if we're surprised by the taste, we'll take mental note of the generic details so that, in the future, we will make even better choices.

Genres should not be construed as fixed categories in heaven, as if our goal is to discover the true definitions of "fruit" and "vegetable" so that we can put the right objects into the right boxes. The fixed point for interpretation is the thing we are interpreting. It is from this and similar things that we abstract our generic categories, which in turn become convenient "tools" for us to use in interpretation. But again, these tools are not fixed. We could easily change our definition of "fruit," join its members with other things to create a new genre (such as organic things), or divide its members to create entirely different generic categories (edible vs. inedible fruits). Genres are flexible categories which help us make sense of and engage the world.

As I've said, the generic process is usually tacit and unconscious. Explicit attention to generic categories is required mainly when we are confronted by what is entirely novel, by something for which our existing categories provide an insufficient basis for comparison and interpretation. When we are confronted by a new or unusual sort of fruit, such as a star fruit or loquat, we attend more closely to comparison. What does it look *like*? What does it smell *like*? Is the skin tough (and probably inedible, *like* a pomegranate) or thin (and perhaps edible, *like* a grape)? How would one go about eating it? *Like* a banana, or a mango, or a peach? This comparative engagement (which focuses on similarities and differences) will advance us towards but will not guarantee gastronomic success. Apart from the advice of wiser fruit eaters, only trial and error will confirm how and what we should eat.

Of course our interest here is not in fruit but in literature. And when it comes to literature, genre is not only a means of interpretation but also of literary production. Just as others can understand our spoken sentences because generic patterns shape our words and grammar, so our larger modes of discourse, such as novels, letters, and histories, are understood because we compose them according to the expected forms. When a text begins with "Once upon a time ..." or "Dear Mary," we instinctively know something about what we are about to read. These texts do not require a heading like "folktale" or "letter." So, generic processes drive both the creation and interpretation of texts. The trick is that this generic transaction is not as simple as interpreting a piece of fruit. Whereas the fruit confirms immediately whether its taste is good or bad, nothing confirms finally that we've successfully read a text, particularly an ancient text. We can easily judge that we've understood it and still be well off the mark. This is why each biblical text yields so many different and often contradictory readings.

Literary genres reflect different strategies for representing reality. The parables of Jesus are a good example. When Jesus said that a Samaritan once turned aside to help his suffering neighbor, he was not referring to a particular Samaritan or neighbor. His parable represented the many instances in which all of us have opportunities to lend a helping hand. Will we fail our neighbor, as the priest and Levite did, or will we come to his aid? That was Jesus' question. And this illustrates well the unique power of fiction. It depicts the broad sweep of human history, and of the human condition, rather than a particular moment in history.

Certainly there are times when detailed, accurate history is called for, but this produces a different kind of representation. When Luke reported that Jesus exited the tomb after his death, he wasn't offering a symbol of our potential for psychological renewal. He intended to say that there was once a particular, very special man named Jesus who died and rose again. Events in history can certainly be described in other ways, as we see in the "little lamb" allegory used by the prophet Nathan to entrap King David (2 Sam 11), but this and similar genres cease to represent reality with similitude, as Luke's gospel did. Nathan's representation was heavy on symbol; Luke's was heavy on similitude. I raise this point because, when we bring our historical questions to the stories in Genesis, we should not confuse *representation in general* with *historical representation*. Historical representation maintains a very close relationship between the narrative and actual events. The flood story in Genesis (as an example) will be this kind of text if and only if the author intended it to represent a literal worldwide flood and a literal boat on which the last vestiges of animal and human life were saved. Anything less will count as representation but not as historical representation.

While it is useful to discern an author's generic strategy for representing reality, we must also ask whether the author's representation is accurate and successful. For example, the author of Genesis claims in the Table of Nations (chap. 10) that there was once a man named Egypt who was the forefather of the Egyptian people. Similar explanations are offered for the origins of many other peoples and nations, such as Canaan and Libya. If we suppose that the author of Gen 10 intended this to describe the actual origins of Egypt, then we'll have to say that he or she was not very successful. To claim that there were once men named Egypt, Canaan, and Libya is a bit like claiming that there were once men named Germany, Italy, and France. Perhaps it was common for ancient ethnographers to postulate national origins in this way, but *adherence to generic convention is not the same thing as reliable representation*. Of course, this generic limitation does not prevent the author of Gen 10 from representing other elements of reality quite well. As we will see later on, the Table offers a splendid window into the social and political world of ancient Israel. So, representation is not a win-or-lose proposition because there are so many ways to "win" in a game that represents reality through texts.

Genesis 1 – 11 as the Word of God

Christians (and Jews) believe that Gen 1–11 is embedded in, and is indeed the introduction to, a larger "canon" of books that together constitute the written word of God. Christians generally agree on the contours of the canon but have never reached full agreement.[5] To this day different branches of the Church include different books and order them in somewhat different ways. In at least one case the disagreement stems from biblical testimony, for the Ethiopic Church, unlike the others, has accepted 1 Enoch as canonical because the author of the Book of Jude accepted it (see Jude 1:14). But that is a matter for another time. Christians on all sides certainly agree that Gen 1–11 is the introduction to and sets many theological agendas for the larger canon from Genesis to Revelation.

It is natural to infer from Scripture's genre, as the Word of God, that there are certain generic traits that cannot appear in its pages. Christian Fundamentalists often deny that the Bible reflects historical error or theological confusion because these traits would ostensibly impugn

---

5. Lee Martin McDonald, *The Biblical Canon: Its Origin, Transmission, and Authority* (Peabody: Hendrickson Publishers, 2007).

God's character. While I am myself an evangelical and understand the strong impulse to stake out this claim, *I don't believe that the Bible's status as the Word of God places any necessary limitation on the range of generic possibilities.* To give just one example, we will see below that the author of Genesis at one point declares a curse on the children of Canaan because his father, Ham, committed a mysterious but apparently egregious sin against Noah (see Gen 9:25). While scholars are not sure what his sin actually was, this understanding of sin and consequence runs afoul of both Ezekiel and Jesus, who taught that God *does not* hold human beings responsible for the sins of their fathers (Ezek 18:20; Jn 9:2–3). This is one of many instances in which the Bible offers diverse viewpoints on the same subjects.[6] How, then, should we think of Scripture?

Scripture is not a room filled with clairvoyant theologians who have the same ideas and agree on every point. It is better understood as a room of wise elders, each an invited guest because of his unique voice and relation to God.[7] Every elder has insight, but no elder has all of the answers, nor are any of them wholly liberated from humanity's broken, sinful condition. Every voice is of value, but each will perhaps push too far in one direction and not enough in another, and each will push, in some way or other, in the wrong direction. When we read Scripture well, we listen in on the conversations of these elders, and, in conversations with other readers, seek as best we can to understand God's voice. It is through this communal reading experience that God points us to his one and only solution for our broken condition: Jesus Christ.[8]

Genesis 1 – 11 as Human Words

God's word is expressed in human languages and generic conventions, so we best honor God's choice to speak in this way by reading Scripture as the human discourse that it is. Many generic categories provide read-

---

6. For a theological discussion of biblical authority in light of biblical diversity, especially biblical violence, see Philip Jenkins, *Laying Down the Sword: Why We Can't Ignore the Bible's Violent Verses* (San Francisco: HarperOne, 2011); Kenton L. Sparks, *Sacred Word, Broken Word: Biblical Authority and the Dark Side of Scripture* (Grand Rapids: Eerdmans, 2012).

7. While I prefer to use gender inclusive language, here and elsewhere in the essay I assume that the biblical authors were men. This is in keeping with the patriarchal perspective of the texts and also with our current understanding of ancient Israelite society, in which scribal education was a male enterprise.

8. For Christ as criterion in biblical interpretation, see John 5:39–40; Ratzinger, *In the Beginning*, 8–18.

ers with a useful grasp on all or parts of Gen 1–11. In what follows I will explore these generic features, beginning with the genealogies in Genesis (because these provided my first "Aha!" moment) before moving on to traits that appear in the text's smaller and larger units. As we pursue this end, we will often consider comparative texts from the ancient Near East and also those within the Bible itself. But in the end, there are no texts from the ancient world that stand generically close in all respects to either the Bible as a whole or to the Book of Genesis. Like all texts, the Bible is ultimately *sui generis*—its own genre.

Genesis 1 - 11 as Primeval History

Anyone with an ounce of curiosity about our life and world will be interested in the first few chapters of the Bible. These combine stories and genealogies to describe the earliest moments of our cosmos and the early days of human history. This is why scholars refer to this part of the Bible as the "primeval history." The basic structure of this history alternates between story and list. The creation story is followed by a genealogical list of the first human beings (who lived much longer than we do), which is then followed by the flood story and by another list of human beings (who, again, lived much longer than we do). If this were the only ancient text we had ever read, it would certainly strike us as quite unique. But for those familiar with other texts from the ancient world, our natural response is a *déjà vu* feeling that we've seen it all before.

The primeval history of Genesis participates in a generic tradition found already in Mesopotamian texts from the third millennium BCE and which endured at least until the time of Berossus in the third century BCE. The basic structure of this tradition, which in whole or part appears in the Eridu Genesis, Sumerian King List, *Atrahasis* and Berossus, is the same as in Genesis: (1) creation, (2) list, (3) flood, (4) list.[9] Some of these texts provide a complete flood story without the full lists (*Atrahasis*) while others provide the lists and only refer to the flood, but again, it's clear that this is how ancient scholars viewed early human history. An important difference between the "list" sections of

---

9. See *ATSHB*, 345–48, 310–11, 313–14, 375–76, respectively. Translations in *ANET*, 265–67, 566–67; BMes, 491–93; *COS* 1.130: 450–52, S. Burstein, *The Babyloniaca of Berossus* (SANE 1.5; Malibu, CA: Undena, 1978).

the Israelite and non-Israelite texts is that the Bible provides a *genealogy* while the Mesopotamian exemplars provide *king lists*. But this key difference aside, the lists share a linear form (one person follows the next) and are chronologically similar. According to the Mesopotamian lists, kings who lived before the flood had especially long reigns (one for 43,000 years), as was true to a lesser extent of kings who lived after the flood (one ruled for 1200 years). The same pattern holds in Genesis, where one pre-flood patriarch lived 969 years (Methuselah) and one after the flood lived 600 years (Shem). The ages are smaller than in the Mesopotamian texts but, as we shall see, no more credible as history.

The aforementioned parallels between the biblical and Mesopotamian primeval traditions are striking and illustrate in general what is also true in more specific cases. As Rembrandt worked in oil on canvas, so the authors of Gen 1–11 worked in the motifs and literary forms of the ancient world.

Genealogy in Genesis 1–11

The primeval history contains four genealogies, one each in Gen 4, 5, 10, and 11. The first and third are segmented in form (a family tree) and the second and fourth are linear in form. Our understanding of these genealogies is best elucidated by examining closely the first two genealogies in Gen 4 and 5. As the table below shows, these two genealogies are actually versions of the same genealogy. The names in the lists are almost identical and are in nearly the same order, but one of the genealogies is now segmented and the other linear. Those familiar with the generic traits of genealogy will not be surprised by this, for genealogies are inherently fluid and are adjusted often to suit new and shifting circumstances.[10] At any rate, it is reasonable to infer that these genealogies were prepared by two different people. This impression is reinforced by other details in the genealogies. Whereas the genealogy in Gen 4 inserts anecdotal family details into a genealogy that lacks chronology, the genealogy in Gen 5 provides extensive chronology but does not include the anecdotes. These differences reflect two different strategies for describing the early days of the cosmos and human history.

---

10. For an overview of the genealogical genres, see *ATSHB*, 354–57; Robert R. Wilson, *Genealogy and History in the Biblical World* (YNER 7; New Haven: Yale University, 1977).

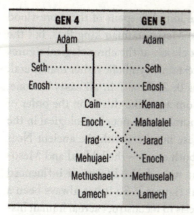

GEN 4	GEN 5
Adam	Adam
Seth	Seth
Enosh	Enosh
Cain	Kenan
Enoch	Mahalalel
Irad	Jarad
Mehujael	Enoch
Methushael	Methuselah
Lamech	Lamech

The author of the first genealogy, in Gen 4, was very interested in the origins of civilization. He or she interspersed in the list various anecdotes about those listed, such as who established the first city, who invented musical instruments, and who first worked in metals. By using a segmented rather than linear genealogy, the author was able to portray humanity as two emerging families with different ethical profiles. One of these yielded the last righteous man, Noah, and the other yielded an increasingly depraved human family, which would finally face destruction. The forefathers of these lineages were Seth and Cain, respectively, each a son of Adam. The religious commitment of Seth's line is accentuated by the claim that during his lifetime the people first "called upon the name of Yahweh" (Gen 9:26). As for Cain's lineage, it begins with a murderer and ends with Lamech, a violent man who boasted about killing unjustly anyone who accidentally injured him (Gen 4:23). Because this author was interested not only in theology but also in interesting details about early humanity, such as the inventors of civilization and founders of cities, let us refer to this author as the "Antiquarian Theologian" (for convenience, the "Antiquarian").

The genealogy in Gen 5 differs from the Antiquarian genealogy not only by virtue of its linear form but also in its subject matter and chronology. The list ends with Israel's forefather, Abraham, and so was written to depict the origins of Israel rather than of humanity in general. For each listed patriarch we are provided with the age at which he had his first child, how long he lived after that, and his age at death. The entry for Seth provides an example:

> When Seth had lived 105 years, he became the father of Enosh. After he became the father of Enosh, Seth lived 807 years and had other sons and daughters. Altogether, Seth lived a total of 912 years, and then he died. (Gen 5:6–8)

We have noted already that the long life spans of these pre-flood biblical heroes has a parallel in the Mesopotamian king lists, but the parallel runs still deeper. If we look closely at the chronological figures in Gen 5, we'll find that these are certainly symbolic rather than literal. The final digit for each number is 0, 2, 5, or 7 in all cases but one. Given that the probability of random ages like this is on the order of .00000006%, it is clear that these numbers are not chronological in the usual sense.[11] A comparison of these numbers with the ancient Near Eastern evidence suggests that in both cases—the biblical and Mesopotamian king lists—the numbers were derived from, or influenced by, astronomical and mathematical figures.[12] So it has always been a mistake to use the lifespans in Genesis to reconstruct actual human history, as Archbishop Ussher once tried to do, and many continue to do.[13] Another similarity between Gen 5 and the Mesopotamian tradition concerns the seventh person in each list. The Mesopotamian king lists often stress the special importance of the seventh king (often Enme-duranki) and his wise advisor (often Utuabzu), who did not die but "ascended into heaven." Genesis 5 also reports that the seventh patriarch was unique: "Enoch walked with God; then he was no more, because God took him" (NRSV).

It is sensible to infer that the author of Gen 5 has created this genealogy by reshaping the genealogy still preserved in Gen 4 (the Antiquarian genealogy). He recast the whole in linear form, added chronology, removed extraneous comments, and inserted a comment about the seventh pre-flood hero. The apparent motive was to create a pre-flood genealogy that looked similar to pre-flood king lists from Mesopotamia. But why would the author have done this?

---

11. The math is relatively simple. One takes the probability of randomly selecting any of the four digits used (i.e., ".4") and raises it to the power equivalent to the number of random selections (18). This yields $.4^{18}$, or 6.87×10^{-8}.

12. C. J. Labuschagne, "The Life Spans of the Patriarchs," in *New Avenues in the Study of the Old Testament: A Collection of Old Testament Studies* (ed. A. S. van der Woude; OTS 25; New York: Brill, 1989), 121–27; Donald V. Etz, "The Numbers of Genesis V 3–31: A Suggested Conversion and Its Implications," *VT* 43 (1993): 171–89; Dwight W. Young, "The Influence of Babylonian Algebra on Longevity among the Antediluvians," *ZAW* 102 (1990): 321–35; idem, "A Mathematical Approach to Certain Dynastic Spans in the Sumerian King List," *JNES* 47 (1988): 123–29; idem, "On the Application of Numbers from Babylonian Mathematics to Biblical Life Spans and Epochs," *ZAW* 100 (1988): 332–61.

13. James Barr, "Why the World was Created in 4004 B.C.: Archbishop Ussher and Biblical Chronology," *BJRL* 67 (1985): 575–608.

For much of Israel's history, especially during and after the Babylonian exile, the Israelites and Jews lived under the oppressive thumb of the Mesopotamian states (Assyria and Babylon) and their imperial heir, Persia. It is common to find in such repressive contexts what anthropologists call "elite emulation."[14] Elite emulation arises when an oppressed culture expresses its identity through the oppressor's images of power. In this case, it appears that Jewish scribes responded to Mesopotamian ideology by composing texts that imitated one of Babylon's most powerful expressions of power: the king list. I and other scholars suspect that the biblical author's motive was to help Jews resist the assimilating pressure of Mesopotamian culture. The stories of Daniel and his friends, and of Esther and Mordecai, suggest that this threat was very real in the exilic and post-exilic period.[15] For this reason, let us refer to the author of the genealogy of Gen 5 as the "Ethnic Apologist" (or the "Apologist").

We have discovered two literary profiles in the genealogies of Gen 4 and 5. Do these profiles also extend to the genealogies in Gen 10 and 11? Indubitably so. The genealogy in Gen 11 picks up where the genealogy in Gen 5 left off and like it, bears a linear form and detailed chronology. Both belong to the Apologist. The fact that the author has extended the genealogy beyond the flood, as the king lists did, provides more evidence that he wanted their genealogy to imitate the older, more venerable Mesopotamian king list tradition. So Israel received a "royal" pedigree.

Only the genealogy in Gen 10 remains to be discussed. The text is customarily referred to as the Table of Nations because it provides a "family tree" of the nations and peoples who lived on the social periphery of ancient Israel. The genealogy must have been edited here and there, for some nations, such as Asshur and Havilah, actually appear in two different places in the Table.[16] So it seems that we cannot assume that the whole of this genealogy was assembled by one person.[17] Nevertheless, the

---

14. See Carolyn R. Higginbotham, *Egyptianization and Elite Emulation in Ramesside Palestine: Governance and Accommodation on the Imperial Periphery* (CHANE 2; Leiden: Brill, 2000); Kenton L. Sparks, "Enûma Elish and Priestly Mimesis: Elite Emulation in Nascent Judaism," *JBL* 126 (2007): 625–48.

15. For discussions, see W. L. Humphreys, "A Life-Style for Diaspora: A Study of the Tales of Esther and Daniel," *JBL* 92 (1973): 211–23.

16. For Asshur, see 10:11, 22; for Havilah, see 10:7, 29.

17. For an overview of the issues and possible solutions, see Claus Westermann, *Genesis: A Commentary* (3 vols.; Minneapolis: Augsburg, 1984–86), 1.495–530.

overall profile of the Table of Nations matches that of the genealogy in Gen 4, which (as we saw) belonged to the Antiquarian. Both genealogies are segmented, attentive to the origins of human culture, and include interesting anecdotes about certain heroes listed in the genealogy.

Much that could be said about Gen 10 will have to go unsaid, but if historicity is our question, then one feature of Gen 10 should be highlighted. The entire genealogy is devoted to the birth of nations, for which the Antiquarianist has employed *eponyms* to account for the origins of each people and nation. (*Eponyms* reflect an ethnographic theory that each nation should be traced back to an ancestor who bore the national name.)[18] Thus, for example, the Antiquarianist tells us that the nation of Egypt was the progeny of a fellow named Egypt, Libya the progeny of Libya, Canaan the progeny of Canaan, and so forth. Anthropologists have observed this ethnographic strategy in many cultures, including ancient Greece. The Catalogue of Women (7th–6th centuries BCE), for example, traces the origins of the Hellanic peoples back to a man named Hellen and the origins of the Hellanic tribes, the Dorians and Aeolians, back to men named Dorus and Aeolus.[19] Of course these nations were not actually birthed by a forefather of the same name, so these genealogical sources should not be consulted for genuine history. But they are very useful if we are interested in how the ancient Israelites, or ancient Greeks, understood themselves in relation to other peoples.

To summarize: the segmented genealogies in the primeval history provided an account of cultural origins and of ancient Israel's relationship to the other cultures. The linear genealogies served in the first instance to express Jewish identity as an alternative to Babylonian identity and, in the second instance, to provide a pedigree for Israel and her Davidic kings by connecting them to hoary antiquity.

Myth in Genesis 1 - 11

Though variously defined, for our purposes "myth" refers to stories in which the gods are major actors and the setting is either in the early cosmos or in the heavens. Readers will immediately have some ideas about

---

18. Laura Bohannan, "A Genealogical Charter," *Africa* 22 (1952): 301–15.

19. The traditional author was Hesiod, though this is disputed. See M. L. West, *The Hesiodic Catalogue of Women: Its Nature, Structure, and Origins* (Oxford: Oxford University Press, 1985), 173.

this genre, envisioning the gods in heaven, talking and fighting, and playing irresponsible games with human history and the like. While this caricature is not wholly out of place, it suggests already that a word of generic caution is in order. Modern readers are quick to assume that "myth" is, in the nature of the case, opposed to "science" and "history," but there is evidence that ancient authors did not think like this. We have recovered a Babylonian scientific text in which Mesopotamian scholars consulted their creation myth, *Enuma Elish*, as a source for their cosmological maps.[20] Egyptian scholarship also reveals a close connection between myth and cosmology and explicitly describes the myths as "that which happened."[21] We must contend as well with the possibility that ancient myth writers sometimes believed their myths to be inspired and hence factually reliable, as the Babylonian priest, Kati-ilani-Marduk, claimed for his Erra Epic.[22] So while we needn't assume in every case that ancient myth writers envisioned a one-for-one correspondence between myth and fact, neither can we presume that they didn't.

If we define myth in this way, then we have in Gen 1–11 two myths in three episodes: the creation in Gen 1 and the paradise/fall story in Gen 2–3. Numerous details reveal that these two myths were not composed at one time by one person. The creation order of animals and human beings differs in Gen 1 and 2,[23] and the method of creation is also different. Whereas in Gen 1 God *speaks* his world into existence, in Gen 2 he plants gardens and fashions humanity out of soil and from a rib. The two myths also use different names for God, *Elohim* in Gen 1 and *Yahweh* in Gen 2. The original ending of the first myth shows that its author did not envision that another myth would immediately follow in Gen 2: "the heavens and the earth were finished, and all their multitude" (Gen 2:1 NRSV). So again, we are reading the myths of two authors. Let us first consider the paradise/fall myth in Gen 2 and 3.

---

20. See the Mesopotamian "Cosmic Geographies" in *ATSHB*, 321–22.

21. For the Egyptian cosmologies, see *ATSHB*, 325–26. For Egyptian descriptions of myth as *ḥprt* ("that which happened") and *gnwt* ("annals"), see Donald B. Redford, *Pharaonic King-List, Annals and Day-Books* (JSSEA Publication IV; Mississauga: Benben, 1986), 86, 92–93.

22. This myth blamed the troubles of Babylon between 1100–750 BCE on the god Erra (also known as Nergel). See *ATSHB*, 319–20.

23. In Genesis 1 the animals are created *before* humanity, but in Genesis 2 they are created *between* the first man and woman.

In our own day, and presumably throughout the drama of history, human beings have experienced the world as a confusing blend of blessing and curse, good and evil, beauty and obscenity. And as a rule, we have a deep sense that this is not how things should be. What is behind this schizophrenic cosmos and our intuition that it's gone awry? The paradise/fall story in Gen 2–3 offers answers for these questions. Here we are told that humanity did not always live in this broken condition. We once lived in a perfect garden, created by God as a safe and peaceful place to enjoy each other and our work. The garden was not ours. It was Yahweh's garden, and we, its gardeners, were permitted to remain there so long as we did not transgress its only law: "You must not eat from the tree of the knowledge of good and evil" (Gen 2:17). Breaking this law would have grave consequences. Not only would we forfeit our idyllic garden home but also our access to the Tree of Life, whose life-renewing fruit protected us from the power of death. Once separated from it, our fate was sealed. Thus, this story indeed tells us why humanity bears in its soul a nagging sense that something is awry. Something wonderful has indeed been lost: humanity contravened the law and ate from the forbidden tree.

Lest we blame Yahweh for our lapse (as Adam and Eve did), the myth explains that the fault did not lie with the creator but entirely with the creatures. The serpent deceived the first couple with lies, and they believed his word rather than God's. Driven by one motive—to acquire divine knowledge—they ate from the forbidden tree. Although the woman succumbed first, and her husband after that, the loss was felt by both and, indeed, by the entire cosmos. Adam and Eve were expelled from the garden, into a world where death was the lot of every person, where the land was cursed, where pain was an ever-present reality, and where the relational harmony between man and wife was broken. And to top it off, humanity lost its intimate life with God in his garden. As terrible as all of this sounds, these were only the birth-pangs of sin in heaven and earth, for still to come were greater human evils and, eventually, the cohabiting of divine beings with human women to produce a mysterious, evil race of Nephilim (Gen 6:4). In this respect, the story of the fall sets the stage for and connects organically with the theme of human sin and hubris that shapes Gen 1–11. Humanity harbors in its heart a misplaced desire for divine knowledge and prerogative.

Numerous motifs in this myth evoke comparison with the Mesopotamian generic traditions. (1) Adam and Eve are "fashioned" from soil by the deity, as in other ancient Near Eastern myths.[24] (2) Humanity is animated by divine potency. While in the biblical story this is applied through "the breath of Yahweh," the common Babylonian agent was divine blood.[25] (3) Divine creation was performed *ex material* by providing shape for the pre-existing but formless earth; we are not dealing here with creation *ex nihilo*, such as we find in the New Testament.[26] (4) The "garden of god" in Eden is comparable to the "garden of the gods" in Mesopotamia, usually understood as a high mountain from which the gods ruled.[27] Given this motif, we should not envision in Genesis an Edenic *world* but rather a more modest garden of Yahweh which was surrounded by the darker, less hospitable world to which Adam and Eve were ultimately banished. The same motif appears in Ezekiel 28, where the King of Tyre is banished from the garden on God's mountain. (5) Adam's role in tilling and keeping the Edenic garden is reminiscent of the work assigned to humans in the Sumerian and Babylonian creation myths. (6) The Tree of Life reminds us of the life-giving *haluppu* plant, which a serpent pilfered from Gilgamesh in the epic that bears his name.[28] (7) Adam and Eve's conversation with the serpent in Genesis sounds very much like an experience of the first Mesopotamian sage, Adapa.[29] The great god Anu offered to Adapa the food and drink of eternal life, but Adapa rejected this because his god, Ea, warned him that this was actually the "bread and water of death." Near the story's end, Anu laments that Ea had revealed to Adapa "the ways of heaven and earth," which is quite close to the "knowledge of good and evil" and "being like God" motifs in Genesis. Many more parallels could be cited, but these make it clear enough that the paradise/fall story stands squarely within the mythic tradition of the ancient world.

---

24. For the motifs of the gods forming humanity and using clay or soil, see the myths of Enki and Ninmaḫ (*ATSHB*, 309), *KAR* 4 (*ATSHB*, 311), Atrahasis (*ATSHB*, 313–14), and the Myth of the King's Creation (*ATSHB*, 321).

25. See *KAR* 4 (*ATSHB*, 311), Atrahasis (*ATSHB*, 313-14), and *Enuma Elish* (*ATSHB*, 314-16).

26. Heb 11:1–3.

27. An early reference to the divine abode is found in the Sumerian "Dispute between Grain and Sheep," where it is referred to as "the hill of heaven and earth" (*COS* 1.180: 575–78).

28. For the Gilgamesh Epic, see *ATSHB*, 275–76.

29. *ATSHB*, 317–19.

Although the biblical author exploited the standard repertoire of mythic motifs and, as in all myths, combined and styled them to advance a particular perspective, the paradise/fall story is especially unique when compared with other ancient exemplars. More so than other myths, this one seems to draw from motifs found in many Mesopotamian exemplars. As I and other scholars see it, this suggests that the author, in order to establish a paradigm for the rest of his history, found it necessary from the outset to craft a completely new myth.[30] The author combined familiar themes from various primeval and creation traditions in order to advance what was, at the time, a profound theological point. Namely, that humanity, from the beginning, was bent on breaking God's law and for this reason lived in perpetual exile, separated from our true home. By advancing this viewpoint, I suspect that the author was situating Judah's exile within the larger context of human brokenness. Both Israel and humanity as a whole have been exiled from their homeland. As the Apostle later expressed it: "All have sinned and fall short of the glory of God" (Rom 3:23). Obviously this implies that this biblical author, although drawing on ancient sources, wrote his history after the Babylonian exile in 586 BCE.[31] This would explain in part the author's intimate familiarity with Mesopotamian literature. The Antiquarian was a true scholar in every sense of the word.

At this point, about halfway through our discussion, I want to suggest a key insight which, I believe, follows from the evidence. *Given the level of creativity in the paradise/fall story, it is very doubtful that the author regarded his myth as historical in the strict sense of the word.* It was a theological composition, steeped in allegory and symbol, which related the story of humanity and not of two individuals only. The fact that later generations of readers have sometimes interpreted these symbolic trees and talking serpent as literal history is not surprising, for, as mentioned above, ancient readers, like those in our own day, often inter-

---

30. Kenton L. Sparks, "The Problem of Myth in Ancient Historiography," in *Rethinking the Foundations: Historiography in the Ancient World and in the Bible, Essays in Honour of John Van Seters* (ed. S. L. McKenzie and T. Römer; BZAW 294 ; Berlin and New York: de Gruyter, 2000), 269–80; Paul Humbert, *Études sur le récit du paradis et de la chute dans Genèse* (Mémoires de l'Université Neuchâtel 14; Neuchâtel: Secrétariat de l'Université, 1940), 7.

31. Scholars commonly date this part of Genesis to the exilic period. See Kenton L. Sparks, *The Pentateuch: An Annotated Bibliography* (IBR Bibliographies 1; Grand Rapids: Baker, 2002), 22–36.

preted myths as "that which happened."[32] For this they can hardly be faulted. And even as we admit that the myth is not strictly factual, let us not infer from this that the author believed nothing of his history. Good metaphors speak of the real world, and ancient writers did not adhere to the neo-classical ideal of "generic purity," which maintained that authors should preserve a firm boundary between history and fiction. The mythmaker would have assumed that a first human couple once existed and that, at some point, their errors resulted in paradise lost. He probably believed as well in the historical veracity of other traditions found in their sources, a matter to be discussed below.

If the creation myth in Gen 2–3 was written by the Antiquarian, it stands to reason that the creation myth in Gen 1 was written by his partner, the Apologist. I believe that the evidence bears this out. As we shall see, the influence of Mesopotamia on the six-day myth in Gen 1 is far more direct than is found in the paradise/fall story, suggesting that here, as in the genealogies of Gen 5 and 11, the author labored to imitate Mesopotamian literature. But first, the story itself.

God spoke the cosmos into existence in only six days. The first few days were devoted to creating the space for life and the remainder to the creation of life itself, of which humanity was the "very good" crowning achievement. The creation of the sun and moon on the fourth day is sometimes taken by modern scholars as a hint that the first three days were not "literal" days, but the author did not need the sun to mark off a literal day and, at any rate, the primary aim was to provide a basis for a Sabbath theology. A literal week was intended because a literal Sabbath was in view. God rested — so must we.

While there are potential connections between this myth and the Egyptian cosmologies,[33] the greater similarity is with the Babylonian traditions, especially with the creation myth, *Enuma Elish*. First, as was common in ancient myths, both texts are introduced with a temporal clause. The biblical myth begins with *Bereshit* ("In the beginning [God created the heavens and the earth]") and the Babylonian myth with *Enuma Elish* ("When on high [heaven had not been named]").

---

32. Redford, *Pharaonic King-List, Annals and Day-Books*, 86, 92–93.

33. As noted by one of the contributors to this volume. See James K. Hoffmeier, "Some Thoughts on Genesis 1 & 2 and Egyptian Cosmology," *JANES* 15 (1983): 39–49.

Secondly, both texts involve creation through separation. In Genesis, God separates the waters above from the waters below, while in the Babylonian myth, Marduk, the city's chief deity, splits in two the watery chaos monster, Tiamat. The monster's name is cognate to the Hebrew word (*tĕhôm*) which Gen 1 uses to describe the sea waters. Third, both myths reflect the existence of heavenly waters, held in place by a dome in the sky.[34] This was a common view in antiquity among scholars and common people alike (as Calvin long ago recognized).[35] Fourth, in both exemplars a heavenly assembly observes the creation of humanity, as we see in Genesis ("Let *us* make humanity) and also in *Enuma Elish* ("Marduk summoned the great gods to Assembly"). Fifth, in both texts humanity is presented as the final and most important achievement in creation, an image reinforced by animating human life through divine power. In Genesis the divine image is bestowed upon humanity, while in *Enuma Elish* humanity is animated by the blood of a rebel god.

While the similarities presented here are often deemed sufficient to secure the relationship between Gen 1 and *Enuma Elish*, there is additional evidence that "seals the deal," as it were. *Enuma Elish* was recited annually on the fifth day of the Mesopotamian New Year festival.[36] On that day, the *kuppuru* ritual was used to cleanse the temple of Marduk from demonic pollution. Do we have any evidence that the biblical authors not only knew *Enuma Elish* but also its *kuppuru* ritual? Absolutely. In Leviticus 16 we find an Israelite ritual that matches the *kuppuru* in name, form, function, and time of year. It is called the *kipper* (from which we get Yom Kippur) and was used at the turn of each year to cleanse Israel's temple precinct. That this Babylonian rite was adopted by the author is suggested not only by these striking parallels but also by obvious evidence that this rite was added to an older ritual in which uncleanness was removed by ritual transfer (using the so-called scapegoat) rather than by ritual detergent (using the *kipper* blood).[37]

---

34. Cf. Gen 1:6–7 and *Enuma Elish* IV.137–147; see also the Egyptian "Book of Nut" (*ATSHB*, 325).

35. John Calvin, *Commentaries on the First Book of Moses called Genesis* (trans. J. King; 2 vols.; Edinburgh: Calvin Translation Society 1847–1850), 1.86–87.

36. For discussion and bibliography, see Sparks, "*Enūma Elish* and Priestly Mimesis," 632–35. For relevant sections of the ritual text, with references to *Enuma Elish*, see *ANET*, 331–34.

37. Sparks, "*Enūma Elish* and Priestly Mimesis."

As in any comparison, the similarities foreground striking differences. The Apologist's creation story is unique because it treats the primeval sea (the *tĕhôm*) as inanimate rather than alive and features a *logos* theology of creation by divine word.[38] These themes reflect the author's commitment to monotheism, which denied the existence of God's heavenly competitors (such as Tiamat) and denied that God should be sullied by forming and shaping dust and blood.[39] In this sense he offers a "demythed" (or less mythical) version of the Babylonian creation story. Equally striking is the Apologist's description of human beings as bearers of the divine image, which breaks markedly with Mesopotamian tradition. While Mesopotamian theology did maintain that human life was animated by divine force, it did not hold that rank-and-file humanity bore the divine image. Common men and women were animated at creation by adding as an active ingredient the blood of a minor deity, usually a rebel deity. If one is looking for the full image of god in humanity, this was found only in the king himself, as we see in the Assyrian coronation prayers and the Neo-Babylonian "Creation of the King" myth.[40] From this we may infer that the Apologist, by bestowing this image on all human beings, wished to present humanity as a whole in royal garb. This impression is reinforced by the author's claim that humanity would "rule" over the creation and also by his genealogies, which mimicked Mesopotamian king lists. The history of the Apologist was strategically shaped from beginning to end to mimic Babylonian tradition. He knew precisely what he was doing.

Tale and Legend in Genesis 1 – 11

Every society tells or writes stories about its past, often more fiction than fact, which then become a part of the cultural lore. Modern scholars attach different labels to these traditional stories, each reflecting certain qualities that appear in or are true of the narrative. Common

---

38. So far as I know, "logos theology" like this appears only in the Egyptian "Memphite Theology" (*COS* 1.15:21–23) and, depending on how one reads it, the Sumerian "Dispute Between Grain and Sheep" (*COS* 1.180:575–578).

39. This author believed in the existence of other divine beings (cf. "Let *us* create man in our image") but did not view them as deities.

40. Sparks, *ATSHB*, 100, 321; W. R. Mayer, "Ein Mythos von der Erschaffung des Menschen und des Königs," *Or* 56 (1987): 55–68; Alisdair Livingstone, *Court Poetry and Literary Miscellanea* (SAAS 3; Helsinki: Helsinki University Press, 1989), 26–27; John Van Seters, "The Creation of Man and the Creation of the King," *ZAW* 101 (1989): 333–42.

labels include "legend," "tale," "novella," and "epic," but there are others. It seems to me that four biblical episodes from the primeval history fit into this broad category of traditional stories: the story of Cain and Abel, the flood story, the curse of Canaan, and the Tower of Babel. These stories were not inspired by history in the straightforward sense, for (as we will see) the first murder was not of a farmer by a shepherd, nor was there ever a world-wide flood, nor did God curse the children of Canaan because his father saw Noah naked, nor is the diversity of human language best explained by divine intervention. All four stories are important, however, for they reflect ancient attempts to explore the issues, questions, and problems that confronted God's ancient people.

The story of Cain and Abel (Gen 4) is closely related to the Antiquarian genealogy of Cain and with it belongs to the author's primeval history. I would describe this story as a "tale," which is my label for short fictional narratives.[41] The fictional character of the story can be deduced from both internal and external evidence. Internal evidence is provided by the names of the characters, Cain and Abel, which are symbols rather than literal names. Cain is the eponymous ancestor of the Kenite nomads and Abel's name is the same word that in Ecclesiastes means "meaningless," an obvious allusion to the brevity of his life.[42] As for the external evidence, the earliest human beings appeared on the scene no later (and perhaps much earlier) than 200,000 years ago and were certainly not engaged in either animal husbandry or horticulture, which first emerged during the Neolithic period (c. 10,000 BCE).[43] So this story of conflict between the first two human children, Abel the shepherd and Cain the farmer, has no early setting and is historically implausible. Still, the story certainly represents the real world, for it was undoubtedly inspired by patterns of violence and jealously which the biblical author observed in human behavior. He adopted as his narrative foil the age-old conflict between shepherds and farmers, as we see in

---

41. As I've indicated already (see "Musings on Genre"), generic labels like "tale" do not have fixed, heavenly definitions. Interpreters invent these categories to facilitate our study and understanding of verbal discourse. For discussion and bibliography on "Tales," see *ATSHB*, 252–70.

42. For the Kenites as Cain's descendants, see Baruch Halpern, "Kenites," *ABD* 4:17–22.

43. Graeme Barker, *The Agricultural Revolution in Prehistory: Why did Foragers become Farmers?* (Oxford: Oxford University Press, 2006).

the much older Sumerian text known as the "Dispute between Sheep and Grain."[44]

The biblical episode was borrowed from some other source, as is suggested by the "sudden" appearance of Cain's wife and other people outside of Eden. But the basic crime-punishment structure of the story is so close to the paradise/fall episode that it must now reflect the editorial hand of the Antiquarian.[45] We can readily see why the story appealed to him. Having portrayed humanity's broken condition in the fall episode, the Antiquarian proceeded to distinguish within humanity two kinds of brokenness, the one, of Adam and Eve, which permitted life in Eden but not in the garden itself, and the other, of Cain, for which even life in Eden was not permitted. The seed of Cain was particularly violent and received a special curse because of it. This violent seed, whose corruption was augmented by the Nephilim, would eventually spread more widely and quickly than Adam's seed, finally resulting in the great flood.

The flood story in Gen 6–9 is longer and more complex than the Cain/Abel story and was perhaps inspired indirectly by an actual catastrophic event. I continue to suspect that the much-discussed "Black Sea Deluge" is behind it.[46] Such a catastrophe could have spawned the belief in a universal flood, which in turn would have inspired explanations for *why* the flood happened and for *how* humanity and animals survived—namely, a giant boat. By the time this story reached the biblical authors, the written flood tradition was already several millennia old.[47] Presumably every scholar in the ancient world (and probably everyone) knew of and believed that the story was true. Because of its relative complexity, dependence on venerable tradition and focus on a cultural hero, I would describe it as a "legend."[48]

We have seen that the Antiquarianist and Apologist sometimes had parallel versions of the same tradition. Did they also have their own versions of the flood story? We know from the Mesopotamian sources that

---

44. *COS* 1.180:575–78; cf. *ATSHB*, 64–65.

45. Westermann, *Genesis*, 1.285–86.

46. Valentina Yanko-Hombach, ed. *The Black Sea Flood Question: Changes in Coastline, Climate and Human Settlement* (Dordrecht: Springer, 2007).

47. Our oldest flood texts date to the second millennium BCE but the Sumerian tradition behind these is older. See *ATSHB*, 310–11.

48. Common definitions of "legend" define it as "a traditional story that treats cultural heroes and institutions." For discussion and bibliography, see *ATSHB*, 271–304.

several editions of the Babylonian flood tradition were floating around among the scribes, so there is no reason why this should not have been the case in ancient Israel as well. And if we look closely at the biblical story, it is quite easy to discern that, indeed, we have in Gen 6–9 two stories that have been combined. Careful readers have long noticed two announcements of the flood, two commands to load animals on the ark (one requires only single pairs of animals and the other seven pairs of clean animals), two different boardings of the ark (seven days before and also on the day of the flood's onset), two different flood chronologies (40 days and one year), and two different divine promises at the story's end (God's promise to never again destroy the earth and the qualified promise never to do this *with a flood*). These parallel elements cohere perfectly with shifts of the divine name from Elohim to Yahweh, such as appear in the two creation stories. So again, we have before us two stories that have been combined. But before we take stock of each story, let us first note their similarities.

Both Hebrew versions of the flood story stand quite close in theme and content to each other and to the older ancient Near Eastern exemplars. The shared motifs include: (1) the divine decision to send the flood as punishment, (2) a warning for the flood hero, including directions to build a huge boat, (3) the flood hero's unique status and symbolic name, (4) a description of the boat's construction, (5) the boarding of the boat by the flood hero's family and earth's animals, (6) the closing of the boat's doors, (7) chronological notices about the flood's duration, (8) the boat's deposit on a mountain top, and (9) divine regret, followed by a resolution never to repeat the flood. As we will see, two other motifs near the end of the story, the bird episode and flood hero's sacrifice, occur in all ancient exemplars except the flood story of the Apologist. The obvious similarities help us foreground the unique perspectives of each biblical author, which can in turn be compared with those of the Mesopotamian versions.

If we compare the flood story of the Antiquarian with the other ancient Near Eastern renditions, the most obvious difference is the author's monotheism. Whereas in the Sumerian and Akkadian legends, one or more gods planned the flood and another divulged it to the flood hero, in the biblical story, Yahweh does double duty as both the planner and revealer of the deluge. Also distinctive is the Antiquarian's reason for the flood. While the Mesopotamian tradition reports that the gods were irritated by humanity's boisterous behavior and destroyed humanity indiscriminately, killing at once both the good and the bad, the Antiquarian attributes the flood more directly to humanity's moral flaws and paints the whole of humanity in dark tones. This is in keeping with the general theme of his contributions to the primeval history. Still, the Antiquarian's portrayal of Yahweh shares the anthropomorphic tendencies of the Mesopotamian tradition. In both cases the deity (or deities) are moved by the flood hero's post-flood sacrifice and, regretting the deed, make a promise to never again destroy humanity. This is, by the way, why the Antiquarian flood story includes seven pairs of clean animals. Without the extra animals his sacrifices would have extinguished several species!

The Apologist's version of the flood story was composed in response to the Antiquarian and ancient Near Eastern flood traditions. His ark did not carry extra animals nor did his flood hero offer a post-flood sacrifice, a detail that distinguished his story from all others.[49] The story ended instead with God's covenant promise to forego further floods and with his covenant sign, a bow in the sky. This was, as the text says, a reminder for God. Although the bow motif is unique within the flood traditions, I do not regard it as entirely novel. The rainbow was a favorable omen in antiquity,[50] and its use in the Bible was inspired by a feature in the Mesopotamian flood stories. I refer here to the colorful lapis lazuli necklace of the goddess Ishtar, which she offered at the end of the flood story as a reminder that the gods should not repeat the offense. This necklace is reminiscent of the Priestly bow in shape, color, and significance.[51] As he does elsewhere in his history, the Apologist has emulated Mesopotamian patterns but has "demythed" them to eliminate their polytheistic profile.

---

49. As scholars have long recognized, this author (known to scholars as the "Priestly Writer") did not permit legitimate sacrifices until the Mosaic tabernacle was built. The best description of this author's work is still Sean E. McEvenue, *The Narrative Style of the Priestly Writer* (AnBib 50; Rome: Biblical Institute Press, 1971).

50. Hermann Hunger, ed. *Astrological Reports to Assyrian Kings* (SAAS 8; Helsinki: Helsinki University Press, 1992), 18, 255.

51. For references in the flood stories of *Atrahasis* and the Gilgamesh Epic, see Stephanie Dalley, *Myths from Mesopotamia: Creation, The Flood, Gilgamesh, and Others* (Oxford: University Press, 1989), 34, 114. For relevant discussion, see Anne D. Kilmer, "The Symbolism of the Flies in the Mesopotamian Flood Myth and Some Further Implications," in *Language, Literature, and History: Philological and Historical Studies Presented to Erica Reiner* (ed. F. Rochberg-Halton; AOS, 67; New Haven, CT: American Oriental Society, 1987), 175-80.

While the Apologist shared the Antiquarian's monotheism, his theology was less anthropomorphic. Whereas the Antiquarian was comfortable with a deity who sends and then deeply regrets a worldwide flood, the Apologist presents God as more emotionally consistent in the transition from a pre- to post-flood world. Everything that God affirmed at creation the Apologist reaffirms after the flood, including God's blessing on humanity, his command that they "be fruitful and multiply," and his declaration that humanity bears the divine image and enjoys dominion over creation (Gen 9:1–7). The Apologist adds to these themes two new laws, one against the consumption of animal blood and the other against homicide. His death penalty for murder is more severe than in the Antiquarian history, which prescribes exile rather capital punishment (cf. Gen 4:12; 9:6). However, the Ethnic Apologist and Antiquarian Theologian do agree on one key point: their flood hero, Noah, does not receive eternal life at the end of the story. The Mesopotamian Flood heroes were always granted this reward.

Immediately after the conclusion of the Antiquarian's flood story we find the famous episode of Noah's drunkenness, which culminates in the curse of Canaan. Although popularly interpreted as evidence that even Noah had his vices, this was not the author's purpose. Noah was the first man to plant a vineyard and so discovered wine's intoxicating power by chance, as was also true in the Persian primeval traditions.[52] The episode clearly reflects the Antiquarian's interest in the invention of cultural arts and professional guilds (in this case, of viticulture) but, as was the case for the story of Cain and Abel, it presumes agricultural practices that were unknown to earliest humanity. Of course viticulture was not the author's primary interest, for the story's central theme was the sharp contrast between Noah's blessing on some of his future children and his curse on the others. While good fortune was pronounced upon Shem's children, the children of Canaan, Noah's grandson, were singled out for a curse because Ham (Canaan's father) was disrespectful to his intoxicated father. This may strike us as unfair, but giving moral lessons is not the point of this story. Rather, it is nothing less than a calculated defense of Israel's right to seize the land of Canaan and slaugh-

---

52. See Mirkhond, *History of the Early Kings of Persia* (trans. D. Shea; London: Oriental Translation Fund of Great Britain and Ireland, 1832), 103–4.

ter all of its people and animals. This has raised deep ethical questions for readers throughout church history, but we cannot address those here.

The Tower of Babel episode is much shorter than the flood story but like it reflects an ancient tradition, in this case that the diversity of human language can be explained by divine intervention. I know of no complete story like this from the ancient Near East, but passing reference is made, in a Sumerian epic, to the role of wise Enki in creating human languages. The text predicts that Enki will eventually restore humanity to one tongue by changing "as many [languages] as he once placed there."[53] Of course traditions of this sort should be appreciated as good exemplars of *ancient scholarship*, but they cannot pass for modern readers as adequate explanations for how and why languages actually develop as they do.

Turning to the Babel story itself, while its language motif is similar to that found in the Enki story and thus reflects the stuff of tale and legend, more is going on in the episode. One biblical scholar has argued persuasively that the tale was directed originally against Sargon II, a Neo-Assyrian king who ruled from 722–705 BCE and was famous in Palestine for conquering Israel and making Judah his vassal.[54] The story parodied Sargon's ambitious building projects, his claim to have united the world with "one speech," and his ultimate failure to complete a palace, which was finally abandoned at Dur-Sharrukin ("Fortresss of Sargon"). If this interpretation is correct (as I and other scholars believe),[55] then it seems that the Tower of Babel story originated as a piece of political resistance to Assyrian occupation. Through a short addition at the end of the story (Gen 11:9), a later scribe then transferred the critique from Assyria to Babylon — in this way creating the so-called "Tower of Babel."

While the Antiquarian inherited rather than composed the Tower of Babel story, the story's original critique of Assyrian and Babylonian arrogance fit very well into his theological scheme. By making a few

53. Herman Vanstiphout, *Epics of Sumerian Kings: The Matter of Aratta* (Atlanta: Society of Biblical Literature, 2003), 65.

54. Christoph Uehlinger, *Weltreich und "eine Rede": eine neue Deutung der sogenannten Turmbauerzählung (Gen 11, 1–9)* (OBO 101; Freiburg: Universitätsverlag, 1990).

55. See also David M. Carr, *The Formation of the Hebrew Bible: A New Reconstruction* (Oxford: University Press, 2011), 245.

minor modifications, the author was able to give it the same "crime and punishment" scheme that appears in his paradise/fall, Cain/Abel, and flood stories. Together these stories convey an important theological message, namely, that hubris is a human flaw that provokes divine judgment. This theme comes through loud and clear in spite of "interruptions" by the voice of the Ethnic Apologist.[56]

Introducing the Anthologist

Two literary profiles are visible in Gen 1–11. While it is possible in theory that a single author could write parallel doublets in a text, perhaps as some sort of stylistic or artistic device, this alone would not explain why the doublets in Genesis present such diverse, even contrary, perspectives on the treated subjects. Why would a single author report that animals were created *before* human beings in Gen 1 and then tell us, in the very next chapter, that animals were created *between* the man and woman? Why would he or she report that Noah entered the ark on the first day of the flood (Gen 7:11–13) and also tell us that he entered it seven days before the flood (Gen 7:1–10)? These questions could go on and on. Genesis was written by at least two people with different ideas about the early days of humanity. This means that someone has combined the parallel stories of the Antiquarian Theologian and Ethnic Apologist into one story, but who?

Some scholars believe that this was done by the Ethnic Apologist himself, who merely inserted additions into the earlier Antiquarian history.[57] One scholar (a contributor to this volume!) believes that this went the other way, with the Antiquarian supplementing the Apologist.[58] While reasonable arguments can be advanced to support these views, I am not convinced that either does justice to the evidence. Differences between the two Hebrew historians are so striking, and their agendas so distinctive, that I cannot believe either would have been satisfied with merely adding his voice to the other. This seems truer still if we look at the rest of the book of Genesis, and the Pentateuch, where we also find

---

56. David J. A. Clines, *The Theme of the Pentateuch* (JSOTSup 10; Sheffield: JSOT, 1978), 61–73.

57. For example, Frank Moore Cross, "The Priestly Work," in *Canaanite Myth and Hebrew Epic* (Cambridge: Harvard University Press, 1973), 293–325.

58. Gordon J. Wenham, "The Priority of P," *VT* 48 (1999): 240–58.

numerous doublets from these two authors.[59] Much more likely is that another writer, less concerned with the particular agendas of the two historians, has combined them into a single book. And this is indeed what most scholars have concluded to be the case.

Generic evidence from the Bible bears this out, for there is another instance in which the scribes wrote parallel histories of ancient Israel. I refer here to the books of Samuel/Kings and the rewritten version of this history prepared by the author of 1 and 2 Chronicles. These twin histories are not wholly comparable to the twin histories in Genesis, but scholars have often noted that the Chronicler and Apologist share very similar, nuanced views of Israel's priesthood and sacrificial rituals. One could for good reasons suggest that they stand together as priestly revisions of earlier Israelite histories. The difference between them is that an editor eventually combined the Apologist's history with its Antiquarian twin, resulting in the book of Genesis and, ultimately, in the Pentateuch.

The unique character of Genesis and the Pentateuch rests especially in its anthological character, for its editor, by combining the two histories, has joined into one collection all of the lore and tradition of early Israel. The result is a staggering variety of generic types, including myth, legend, fable, folktale, novella, history, chronology, etiology, ritual descriptions, ritual prescriptions, genealogy, king list, oath, treaty, and ethical will. The editor so valued tradition, and was so fixed on collecting these sources, that he or she did not care (or did not care much) about whether the traditions fit together nicely. In this respect the editor's temperament shaded in the direction of the Egyptian priests at Edfu, who inscribed in one text a series of "contradictory" versions of how the god Horus defeated Seth.[60] A modern historian, he was not.

Because of his impulse to collect in one document the lore and traditions of Israel, I would describe the editor of Genesis as the Anthologist and his work, the Pentateuch, as an *ethnic anthology*.

---

59. We find in Genesis two (or three) versions of the Abrahamic covenant and, in the story of Jacob which follows, two departures from Palestine, two reasons for the departure, two destinations for his trip, two occasions in which the town of Bethel is named, two occasions in which Jacob is renamed Israel, and two returns of Jacob to Palestine. We could easily extend this list if we included the Pentateuch's other books.

60. *ATSHB*, 328.

Conclusions

Historical questions arise naturally for readers of Genesis. Long before modern science made the gap between Eden and our world crystal clear, Christian scholars like Origen balked at the idea that Genesis was literal history, regarding as "altogether blind" those who thought otherwise.[61] This produced equal and opposite responses from other Christians, such as Ephrem the Syrian, who believed in the complete historicity of Genesis.[62] As Qohelet said, "There is nothing new under the sun" (1:9). Debates like this reflect an intuitive if not rational sense that the historicity of the text—or lack thereof—has some bearing on how we understand its discourse as a human voice and, ultimately, as God's voice. Our questions do not guarantee right answers. But it is far better to ask and err than to assume naively that the text is something it isn't.

Historical queries have often conflated several closely related issues into one. In the foregoing I have tried to tease out these issues by focusing on three different questions: (1) Did the biblical authors intend at every point to write historically reliable narratives? (2) Did the authors believe that history stood behind their narratives? (3) Did the authors accept as history anything which cannot in fact be historical?

Did the authors intend at every point to write reliable history? As I see it, the answer must be no. Our comparison of the texts and sources reveals pretty clearly that the authors were so invested in shaping and reshaping their sources that they cannot have intended their work to yield similitude with actual events. The Antiquarian knew that serpents do not talk. In saying this, I don't intend to suggest that the authors were avoiding history, as might be the case in full-fledged allegory. I mean instead that they were so busy doing something else that historical questions were not in the foreground of their thinking.

Did the authors believe that history stood behind their narratives? Surely they did, though the answer will not be the same for all parts of the narrative. While it is unlikely that the Apologist believed in a literal

61. Origen, *de Principiis*, 4, 16. See Alexander Roberts and James Donaldson, eds. *Ante-Nicene Fathers* (10 vols.; Buffalo: Christian Literaure Publishing, 1885), 4.365.

62. Ephrem the Syrian, *Commentary on Genesis*, 1.1. See Edward G. Mathews Jr. trans., *The Fathers Of The Church: A New Translation, v. 91* (Washington: Catholic University of America, 1994), 74.

six-day creation and even less likely that the Antiquarian believed in a literal garden with trees, there can be little doubt that both believed in one God who created our world, that there was a primal human couple, and that humanity was creation's crowning achievement. Both authors would have accepted as historical the basic contours of the flood story—the boat, animals, and the flood hero—but they were not so transfixed with history that this prevented them from reshaping the story to advance their theological messages.

Did the authors accept as history anything which cannot in fact be historical? In some cases they did, with the flood story being the poster child. Everyone in antiquity seems to have believed that this deluge took place because they were not privy to the insights of modern geology and evolutionary biology. On this score the biblical authors should not be faulted. We should extend to them the same grace if they believed in eponymous ancestry and the confusion of languages at Babel. We will look as confused in a thousand years as they do now.

If we have learned anything from our generic engagement with Gen 1–11, it is that this text and its elements participated fully in ancient generic traditions that could never yield dependable history or modern science. Rather than allow ourselves to be distracted by these limitations, we will do far better if we honor the humble medium of Scripture and try, as best we can, to listen to what the ancient authors were trying to say through that medium. Humanity will not be saved by accurate historical recollections or scientific facts. We are saved through God's actual intervention in our world through the person of Jesus Christ. Gen 1–11, when read well, points us to him.

RESPONSE TO KENTON L. SPARKS

JAMES K. HOFFMEIER

The title of Kenton Sparks' essay, "Genesis 1–11 as Ancient Historiography" gives one the impression that the reader would be treated to a serious comparative study of ancient Near Eastern (ANE) historiography and Gen 1–11. That expectation, however, was not met. Instead, Sparks produced an ideological essay in which mythology seems to be the driving force in ANE historiography. He further tips his hand early on in his paper that reveals his approach to Gen 1–11, viz. that current scientific theory is the ultimate authority to which the reader of Scripture must defer. He finds support for this priority by appealing to Augustine and Aquinas who cautioned against interpreting Scripture in a way that the non-believer would ridicule, quoting the latter: "(Christians) should adhere to a particular explanation [of Scripture] only in such measure as to be ready to abandon it, if it be proved with certainty to be false; lest Holy Scripture be exposed to the ridicule of unbelievers, and obstacles be placed to their believing" (p. 110).

It is hard to disagree with the position that one's interpretation of Scripture should not be verifiably false. My problem is that whenever there is a conflict between the two, Sparks rarely gives Genesis the benefit of the doubt; science is always right, never to be questioned. In that light it is salutary to balance the above quote of Aquinas with another of his affirmations that demonstrates that when human knowledge and Scripture come in conflict, revealed truth supersedes human science and reasoning.

> Holy teaching assumes its principles from no human science, but from divine science, by which as by supreme wisdom all our knowledge is governed.... What is peculiar to this science's knowledge is that it is about truth which comes through revelation, not through natural reasoning.[63]

---

63. St. Thomas Aquinas, *Summa Theologiae* (trans. Thomas Gilby; New York: McGraw-Hill, 1964), 1:23.

The major obstacle for Sparks that precludes reading Gen 1–11 as "straightforward history" are the developments in science, especially evolutionary biology and genetics. The Bible's report that Adam and Eve were directly created by God (Gen 1:26–28 & 2:7ff.) does not fit what current anthropology and DNA studies teach about human origins. Furthermore, he sees a contradiction between Gen 4's portrayal of Cain and Abel as being culturally Neolithic—that is, a farming and sheep herding culture—and how human development is now understood in light of anthropological data. The Neolithic revolution, as it is often called by archaeologists, saw human development transition from the hunter-gatherer stage (Paleolithic culture) to the Neolithic period that began in the Fertile Crescent in the eighth to seventh millennia BC[64] and as early as the eleventh or tenth millennium BC in Anatolia.[65] Neanderthal and Cro-Magnon man date several hundred thousand years prior to the Neolithic era.

He continues, "There was no Edenic garden, nor trees of life and knowledge, nor a serpent that spoke, no worldwide flood in which all living things, save those on a giant boat, were killed by God" (p. 111). For him, scientific developments make it impossible to hold these biblical stories as "literal history that our Christian forbears assumed [it] to be" (p. 111).

The second obstacle for Sparks embracing the Gen 1–11 narratives as representing real events is his view of the nature of the literature itself. Appropriately he declares:

> There are no texts from the ancient world that stand generically close in all respects to either the Bible as a whole or to the Book of Genesis. Like all texts, the Bible is ultimately *sui generis*—its own genre. (p. 117)

Here may be one place where I concur. While there are many types of ANE literature that elucidate our reading of Genesis, there is nothing precisely like it. While Sparks acknowledges that the book of Genesis, and Gen 1–11 in particular, is a unique body of literature (i.e. its *sui*

---

64. One of the earliest Neolithic villages in Mesopotamia was Jarmo in northern Iraq. See Patty Jo Watson, "Jarmo," in *OEANE* 3, 208–9. For this development in Egypt, see Michael Hoffman, *Egypt Before the Pharaohs* (London: ARK Paperbacks, 1984), chapters 4–6.

65. Ronald Gorny, "Anatolia, Prehisotric," *OEANE* 1, 122–24.

generis nature), in the end, he does not treat Gen 1–11 that way. Instead he concludes that the stories vary in genre, but are, following ANE genres that included myth, legend, and tales and that most of the early Genesis narratives are borrowed from Mesopotamia models during the Babylonian exile.

Sparks' methodology is self-evident. Science tells us what we can believe. This reflects a *Wissenschaft über alles* (i.e. science triumphs over all!) world-view and approach to his reading of Gen 1–11. This approach is patently an Enlightenment or modern worldview where reason always trumps revelation (contrary to Aquinas!), the natural overrides the supernatural, and science reduces God to a passive actor if that. As a consequence of his questionable assumption, Sparks is obliged, then, to find literary categories (genres) in Gen 1–11 that result in dismissing these narratives as reflecting reality. Genesis 1–11, nevertheless, for Sparks should be read only for its theological message as if theology has nothing to do with actual events.

The following critique will be divided into the two areas identified here: science (Scripture and interpretation) and genre (literature and history).

Science (Scripture and Interpretation)

To a point, I am sympathetic with Sparks' concern that one's interpretation of Scripture be responsible, and I would add, within the bounds of exegetical possibilities and ought not be needlessly embarrassing. The problem with allowing science to be the final arbiter of what can be accepted as real and authentic in Gen 1–11 is that such a hermeneutic requires one to question even more bedrock Christian doctrines. The resurrection of Jesus is a case in point. Paul found that out in presenting the gospel to the philosophical elites of Athens: "When they heard of the resurrection of the dead, some mocked" (Acts 17:32). Paul's response was not to change the gospel because people could not intellectually accept the crucifixion and resurrection. Rather, he acknowledged that the "Christ crucified" was "folly to Gentiles" (1 Cor 1:23).

Then one must ask, by what biological law or principle can the incarnation of Jesus Christ, his virgin birth, and his death followed by his resurrection on the third day be explained? Nevertheless, as Paul argues, the hope of resurrection of the believer is tied to that of Jesus (1 Cor 15:16–19). This demonstrates that if one accepts the *Wissenschaft über alles* hermeneutic that there are extremely serious problems for the central tenants of Scripture embraced by orthodox Christianity. The resurrection, then, fails both the "ridicule" and scientific (biological) tests, and so the same interpretive principle espoused by Sparks for Gen 1–11 should lead him to jettison the historicity of the resurrection.

The problem science poses for the resurrection notwithstanding, Sparks accepts Luke's testimony about the resurrection to be sober history. Given his penchant for uncritically accepting the "assured results" of critical biblical scholarship, one wonders why he does not follow the positions of New Testament scholars like Rudolf Bultmann, the Jesus Seminar, and Bart Ehrman who do not consider Luke to be writing straightforward history!

Throughout his paper, Sparks regularly identifies an interpretive problem in the text when viewed against science, and sees the only solution to be a revisionist reading of Scripture. In my judgment, he creates false dichotomies as if only two options are possible, literal history or fiction. He claims that "the first chapters of Genesis ... certainly do not offer ... a literal account of events that actually happened prior to and during the early history of humanity" (p. 111). There are, as a result, two camps: those who embrace science and read the Bible in that light, or the biblicists, fundamentalist Christians who reject science in order to preserve their literalistic hermeneutic. What educated Christian would want to fall into the latter group? The problem, apparently as Sparks sees it, is that if one accepts the findings of science that one has to reject, among other things, a historical Adam: How do I know? The DNA tells me so!

Similarly, Sparks insists that a straightforward reading of Gen 1 requires a six-day creation, whereas science suggests a protracted period that took eons. Once again the reader is forced to make a hard choice, science or Scripture. Here too Sparks unnecessarily creates false dichotomies. As a matter of fact, for nearly forty years of teaching at Christian colleges and the seminary where I presently teach, I have never advocated literal six-day creation and young earth.

In recent years, biblical scholars,[66] including evangelicals,[67] have read Genesis with more nuance and literary sensitivity and in the light of ancient Near Eastern cosmological texts. Johnny Miller and John Soden, known for their conservative Christian credentials and once adherents to a young earth theory, have recently written a compelling book entitled *In the Beginning ... We Misunderstood*.[68] Based on their reading of Gen 1 comparatively with ANE cosmologies and aware of the developments in science, they no longer hold to a young earth, recent creation, and a literal six-day creation. This book well illustrates that evangelicals are not stuck in pre-scientific modes of thinking about the Genesis creation narratives.

Do the recent understandings of human genetics and evolutionary biology require one to reject a historical Adam and Eve, Eden, and fall as Sparks believes? No. In fact, there are evangelical OT scholars who accept varying degrees of human evolution, while maintaining a historical Adam.[69]

Human evolution and the biological sciences are by nature descriptive. They cannot tell us *what* caused or *who* made it happen, and *what* or *who* made matter and transformed inanimate material living to organisms. Even if one recognizes that biological evolution occurred, the Bible demands that we view this as *how* God created. God is the *who* behind the processes and he sovereignly controls them creating according to his will. Scripture answers the real questions the humans long to have answered.

It seems to me that an evangelical could accept the view that God the creator did his work over time, relishing in his work as the master artisan as the language of Gen 1 and 2 suggest, while the angels "shouted for joy" at his handiwork (Job 38:7), and that God possibly took a human or hominid (with genetic links to earlier forms of life) and made him the first true "man" (*'ādām*), made uniquely in the image

---

66. Mention was made of studies by Gary Rendsburg, Isaac Kikiwada, and Patrick Quinn in my chapter above.

67. Gordon Wenham's commentaries and articles cited in my chapters above are one excellent example, and we can add the numerous works of John Walton, e.g. *Genesis 1 as Ancient Cosmology* (Winona Lake, IN: Eisenbrauns, 2011).

68. Johnny Miller and John Soden, *In the Beginning ... We Misunderstood* (Grand Rapids: Kregel, 2012).

69. See essays in *Four Views on the Historical Adam* (eds. M. Barrett & A. Caneday; Grand Rapids: Zondervan, 2013). For a review of recent theories, see C. John Collins, *Did Adam and Eve Ever Really Exist?* (Wheaton: Crossway Books, 2011), 121–31.

and likeness of God (Gen 1:26–27; 5:1b–2; 9:6b), and thus a special creation! Such an approach does not militate against a historical Adam whose way of life is described as Neolithic.

This man and his wife (Eve) may be archetypal, that is representative of humanity, but that does not make them an unhistorical couple. If so, then we would have to conclude that Luke got it all wrong in trying to connect Jesus ("being the son [as was supposed] of Joseph) all the way back to Adam (Luke 3:23–38). And so did Paul who made important theological points based on Adam's sin (the fall) that humans die, but how in Christ sinful humans can live again (1 Cor 15:22 & 45).

From a New Testament perspective, Gen 3 is more than a fictive etiology. For Sparks, however, "This story indeed tells us why humanity bears in its soul a nagging sense that something is awry. Something wonderful has indeed been lost: humanity contravened the law and ate from the forbidden tree" (p. 124). At the same time, however, Sparks asserts that it is "Less likely that the Antiquarian [i.e. the source behind Gen 2–3] believed in a literal garden with trees" (p. 139). For him, "The paradise/fall story stands squarely within the mythic tradition of the ancient world" (p. 125) while at the same time, this "story indeed tells us why humanity bears in its soul a nagging sense that something is awry. Something wonderful has indeed been lost." Where does this nagging sense come from? How is it that humans sense that something has been lost if they never had it in the first place? And why should the believer have the hope of restoring the broken fellowship with God and once again have access to the tree of life that never existed, even though Ezekiel anticipated a future access to this tree and its fruit and "leaves for healing" (Ezek 47:12). The same tree is also pictured in the new heaven and earth in Revelation 22. There the Edenic "river of the water of life" flows from God's throne and tree of life with its healing leaves is present (Rev 22:1–2). It seems implausible to me that there can be an eschatological hope without the archetype of Gen 2.

Genre (Literature and History)

The reader of the Bible must pay careful attention to the nature of the literature, and I would agree that the genre is a critical factor on how one understands and interprets a passage. While the Christian reader of Gen 1–11 must be sensitive to the nature of the literature, he or she must bear in mind Aquinas's aforementioned position that, with regard to Scripture, "it is about truth which comes through revelation, not through natural reasoning."[70]

Sparks' literary approach to Gen 1–11 represents one of the most radical wing of Old Testament critical scholarship. He seeks to masquerade the fact that he embraces a source critical approach to the Pentateuch by calling the main sources of Gen 1–11 as the Antiquarian, Apologist, and the Anthologist. Behind the masks of his imaginary friends are Wellhausen's Jahwist (J), the Priestly writer (P), and the editor/redactor.[71] Rather than follow the classical view that dates J to the tenth century, Sparks follows the ultra-late date for J, viz. the period of the exile. It is an amazing coincidence, or is it (?), that Sparks dates J to the exilic period as advocated by his teacher and mentor, John Van Seters.[72]

Here is not the place for a full-blown discussion of source criticism, although in my chapter I did sketch out some recent trends in OT scholarship that have moved away from source critical approaches. An essay by the post-modern OT scholar, David Clines, lampoons the traditional Wellhausenian approach of biblical scholarship.[73] In "New Directions in Pooh Studies," Clines offers a tongue-in-cheek reading of "Winnie-the-Pooh," hereafter abbreviated W, containing traditions of higher antiquity than the Deutero-Pooh book, "The House at Pooh Corner."[74] Utilizing the different names for Winnie-the-Pooh (including Pooh and Bear), he determines (following one criterion used by

---

70. Aquinas, *Summa Theologiae*, 1:23.

71. For clarifications on these identities, see Kenton Sparks, "The Problem of Myth in Ancient Historiography," in *Rethinking the Foundations: Historiography in the Ancient World in the Bible, Essays in Honour of John Van Seters* (eds. S.L. McKenzie & T. Römer; Berlin: de Gruyter, 2000), 269–80.

72. In his essay in this volume, Sparks does not explicitly attach dates to his sources, but he clearly places the borrowing and adapting of Mesopotamian myths by the "biblical author" "to help Jews resist the assimilating pressure of Mesopotamian culture" (p. 121). See explicitly his dating of the origins of Genesis 2–3, in Sparks, "The Problem of Myth in Ancient Historiography," 277–80. For Van Seters' view on down-dating J, see *Abraham in History and Tradition* (New Haven: Yale University Press, 1975) and *Prologue to History: The Yahwist as Historian in Genesis* (Louisville: Westminster/John Knox Press, 1992).

73. David Clines, "New Directions in Pooh Studies: Überlieferungs-un Religionsgeschichtliche Studien zum Pu-Buch," in *On the Way to the Postmodern: Old Testament Essays* (2 vols.; Sheffield: Sheffield Academic Press, 1992), 2:830–39.

74. Ibid., 2:830.

OT scholars to isolate sources in Genesis, i.e. divine names) that W version there is "a plain indication of the interweaving of a number of sources," whereas in the P(ooh)-corpus, other names are used: Edward Bear, Winnie-*ther*-Pooh, P. Bear, and Sir Pooh de Bear.[75] This irreverent reading of Milne's writings is intended to poke fun at adherents of Wellhausen's Documentary Hypothesis who are so certain that they cannot only identify and isolate sources in Genesis, but can date them without any external corroborating evidence.

Another problem I have with Sparks' essay has to do with his approach to historiography that sees mythology as a major component. He rightly acknowledges the challenge of defining myth, but he settles on one that is radically different than that of the phenomenologists of religion that I champion. In fact, I am somewhat confused by his use of myth, because he has elsewhere thought carefully about this literary category, and recognizes one type as "historical myths" in which "the events actually happened."[76] While it is unclear why he does not use this classification on Gen 1–11, it may be due to his deference to science.

Concerning historiography, history writing, volumes have been written on the relationship between ANE historiography and the OT during the past thirty years.[77] The school of thought followed by Sparks[78] is that of Van Seters, which is heavily influenced by Greek ideas of historiography, which utilized myth and legend.[79]

What concerns me about Van Seters' (and Sparks') understanding of historiography is that it embraces western (Greek) approaches to history as an improvement on those of ANE, which is why Sparks repeatedly speaks of the episodes of Gen 1–11 as not writing "reliable history," "cannot in fact be historical," "dependable history," and of an Egyptian

---

75. Ibid., 2:830–31.

76. Sparks, "The Problem of Myth in Ancient Historiography," 270–76, quote on p. 274.

77. For a review of the main works that appeared in the 1970s, see James K. Hoffmeier, *Israel in Egypt* (New York: Oxford University Press, 1996), 10–13. For an evangelical interaction with the literature of the 1970s through the early 1990s, see essays in *Faith, Tradition and History: Old Testament Historiography in Its Near Eastern Context* (A.R. Millard, J.K. Hoffmeier & D.W. Baker; Winona Lake, IN: Eisenbrauns, 1994).

78. In his contribution to this volume Sparks does not overtly associate his approach with that of Van Seters, but he does in footnote 31 cite his own article "The Problem of Myth in Ancient Historiography," and there his concurrence with Van Seters' assumptions and conclusions.

79. John Van Seters, *In Search of History: Historiography in the Ancient World and the Origins of Biblical History* (New Haven: Yale University Press, 1983), 8–54.

writer, "a modern historian, he was not" (p. 137). All of this suggests that ancient Near Eastern writers, including the biblical authors, lacked the critical and objective faculties of the modern historian. The reality is that increasingly modern historians, especially of the post-modern schools of thought, are not writing objective history, but revisionist versions to suit their political agendas. Historian Keith Windschuttle's book is clarifying on this point, as the title reveals: *The Killing of History: How Literary Critics and Social Theorists are Murdering Our Past*.[80]

I would argue that there is no single historiographic genre or way of writing about a nation's past. It could be written in a sober annalistic style, as an epic poem, or as a family genealogical history as I have proposed for Genesis. The present-day western historian simply cannot dictate to an ancient culture how they should record their history.

Nearly two-thousand years ago Josephus responded with alarm to the elevation of Hellenistic approaches to history writing over those from the Near East.

> My first thought is one of intense astonishment that the current opinion that, in the study of primeval history, the Greeks alone deserve serious attention, that the truth should be sought from them, and that neither we (the Jews) nor any others in the world are to be trusted. In my view the very reverse of this is the case,... the Egyptians, the Chaldeans, and Phoenicians ... possess very ancient and permanent record of the past.[81]

Josephus's protest is a cautionary note to those today who think that the Greek (western) historiographic tradition is trustworthy while those of the Near East and Israel were not. This strikes me as unnecessarily Euro-centric.

I welcome Sparks' position that Gen 1–11 is ultimately theological in nature and that it points to Christ. Given his belief that most of these narratives were based on borrowing Mesopotamian myths and legends during the exile and reshaping them (Gunkel's idea of Hebraizing), it seems counterintuitive to think that exilic monotheistic Jewish writers

---

80. Keith Windschuttle's, *The Killing of History: How Literary Critics and Social Theorists are Murdering Our Past* (San Francisco: Encounter Books, 1996).

81. Flavius Josephus, *Against Apion* (trans. H. St. J. Thackeray; LCL; Cambridge: Harvard University Press, 1926), 1.6–8.

borrowed fictive pagan stories to establish their cosmology and pre-history. As I argued in my paper in this book, however, what we see in the book of Daniel is resistance to the polytheistic practices of the Babylonians, not acquiescing to it.

It is a stretch to believe that these borrowed fictive myths and legends somehow are transmogrified into pointers to Christ! A final consequence of Sparks' position on Gen 1–11 is that the cloud of witnesses in Hebrews 11 has shrunk; Abel, Enoch, and Noah never existed!

RESPONSE TO KENTON L. SPARKS

GORDON J. WENHAM

I should like to begin my response to Kenton Sparks by reaffirming what I said to James Hoffmeier, namely that in our understanding of the message of Gen 1–11 we are in substantial agreement. Sparks offers a fine reading of the fall narrative on pages 124–25 with which I resonate strongly. He also sets out clearly his understanding of some of the key terms in this discussion, such as legend, tale, and myth. He writes with a vivid and engaging style that makes for a stimulating read.

But whether it is a valid reading of Gen 1–11 is another matter. Sparks not only accepts the discoveries and theories of modern science, he also endorses wholeheartedly the hypotheses of late nineteenth-century biblical criticism, and he states his views with such dogmatism that the ordinary Bible student might well conclude that these ideas were proved beyond question. Among the dubious hypotheses endorsed by Sparks are: that the genealogies in Gen 4 and 5 are alternative versions of the same genealogy, that the flood story in Genesis combines two versions of the account, that the Tower of Babel story reflects the building efforts of Sargon II, and that the Pentateuch reflects pressures on the Jews during the exile.

These were the sort of theories bandied around when I was a student: we were told that they were the "assured results of criticism." But in subsequent decades these results have all been questioned by some of the most eminent scholars in the field of Old Testament study.[82] For example, Norman Whybray, in *The Making of the Pentateuch*,[83] tore apart the arguments in favor of the Documentary Hypothesis. He

---

82. For a review of debates in pentateuchal studies see Gordon J. Wenham, "Pondering the Pentateuch: the Search for a New Paradigm," in *The Face of Old Testament Studies* (ed. Bill T. Arnold and David W. Baker; Grand Rapids: Baker Books, 1999), 116–44.

83. R. Norman Whybray, *The Making of the Pentateuch: a Methodological Study* (Sheffield: JSOT Press, 1987).

pointed out how defenders of the theory try to have their cake and eat it: they claim on the one hand that consistency is the mark of a source, but when sources are combined the resulting document may exhibit disunity. Sparks argues similarly in his discussion of the Anthologist (p. 136–37). On the European continent, Rolf Rendtorff set a new trend in criticism arguing that texts grew by gradual accretion not by weaving together independent sources.[84] Meanwhile, Jewish literary experts such as Robert Alter[85] and Meir Sternberg[86] emphasized the importance of interpreting the final form of the text, not putative earlier versions. They showed how repetition and apparent contradictions were not to be understood as proofs of multiple sources but as gateways into the subtler nuances of the author. Hoffmeier is aware of these trends, but Sparks ignores them.

I would argue that in the light of this diversity of critical opinion that dogmatism is out of place. But there is another trend in modern thought that should lead us to be cautious: postmodernism. Postmodernism has highlighted the subjectivity and relativism of scholarship. Taken to an extreme, postmodernism leads to the conclusion that there are no absolutes: truth and meaning are the creation of the reader or interpreter. This is taking the idea too far.[87] But it is certainly correct to recognize that the reader has a big input to interpretation, so we should make modest claims about our interpretations and their probability. We must not describe possibilities as certainties.

This is especially the case when appeal is made to the process of composition to illuminate the meaning of a text. Sparks does this repeatedly. For example, he argues that the genealogy of Seth has been created by its author (the Apologist = P) from the genealogy of Cain in Genesis by the Antiquarian (= J). The evidence for this process is slight: the names come in a different order and only two names are identical. The other names are quite distinct, but Sparks exaggerates their similarity to justify his theory. Sparks holds these changes were

84. Rolf Rendtorff, *The Problem of the Transmission of the Pentateuch* (Sheffield: JSOT Press, 1990).

85. Robert Alter, *The Art of Biblical Narrative* (New York: Basic Books, 1981).

86. Meir Sternberg, *The Poetics of Biblical Narrative* (Bloomington: Indiana University Press, 1985).

87. For a helpful discussion see Kevin J. Vanhoozer, *Is There a Meaning in This Text?* (Grand Rapids: Zondervan, 1998).

made to make the genealogy more like the Mesopotamian king lists. Why and when did the "Apologist" (P) do this? Sparks surmises that it occurred during the Babylonian exile to cheer up the Jews living there. That the Jewish kings also had an ancient pedigree is the message of Gen 5 according to Sparks. But if one asks what the evidence is for this historical reconstruction, there is precious little. We do not know that the author of Gen 5 based his work on Gen 4. We certainly do not know whether he wanted to imitate the Babylonian king list. The only definite fact is that the Jews were exiled to Babylon, but whether Genesis was written there is quite moot. In other words, this reconstruction is speculative guesswork. It cannot provide a firm basis for determining the genre of Gen 1–11 or even the genre of just chapters 4 and 5.

But as I argued in discussing Hoffmeier's work, we should not be relying on understanding the creative process to determine the genre of the text. Rather, we need to look at the final finished product. Thus in chapter 5 the genealogy has ten members from Adam to Noah, whereas chapter 4 has seven members, from Adam to Lamech. Apart from Adam who naturally figures in both as the father of both Cain and Seth, the lists have only two names in common, Enoch and Lamech. To make sure we do not confuse Enoch descended from Cain with Enoch descended from Seth, or confuse the two Lamechs, Genesis mentions their different achievements. Enoch (Cain) was involved with building a city. Enoch (Seth) walked with God. Similarly Lamech (Cain) was famed for his bigamy and violence, whereas Lamech (Seth) blessed his son Noah. Enoch and Seth are the only two patriarchs in Gen 5 to have such comments made about them. The other patriarchs listed are just names in the genealogy. Far from Gen 5 being created out of Gen 4, these comments underline the difference between the two lines of descent from Adam. It is as if to say: this Enoch is different from the one in 4:17–18 and this Lamech is not the same as the brutal man in 4:19–24. Set alongside each other the two genealogies trace the development of the two types of humanity, the worldly-wise and sometimes violent line of Cain and the godly line of Seth, bearer of the divine image, which included such saints as Enoch, Lamech, and Noah, two of whom "walked with God."

Like Hoffmeier, Sparks draws on the Gilgamesh/Atrahasis accounts of the flood to illuminate the particular slant on the tale that Genesis gives it. This is helpful and valid in my opinion, though Sparks does also stress the similarities. But I think an ancient oriental hearing the Genesis version for the first time would not be struck by the similarities. He would take them for granted. It is the differences that would surprise him: its monotheism (only one God!), God's total sovereignty over the elements, his anger at sin, his rewarding of obedience and so forth.

But once again Sparks relies on the surmise that Gen 6–9 is composed of two sources, at the cost of failing to note the differences between some of the alleged doublets. For example, Noah is first given a warning of what is going to happen and told to make an ark and to store food on the ark. Later he is told to board the ark with the animals. To say these are two commands to board the ark is to miss the development in the plot. Sparks reads his reconstructed sources separately, arguing that they have different concerns. If there were really two independent sources this procedure might have some validity. But I have indicated my doubts. If Sparks' approach were correct, it would still miss the contribution of the combined final account. Consequently, Sparks makes nothing of the connection between the violence filling the earth before the flood and the institution of capital punishment for murder after the flood. Another overarching theme is that of de-creation/re-creation. The first creation is destroyed in the flood and the earth is covered in water just as it was in the beginning (Gen 1:2). When the wind of God blows (8:1, cf. 1:2) the waters subside, the dry land appears, plants are seen and the animals emerge to repopulate the earth. Creation is restored. A new beginning is possible. Noah and his wife are the new Adam and Eve, from whom all mankind is descended. Noah is described as perfect (blameless, ESV) in 6:9 (cf. 7:1), so all looks rosy for the future of the human race. But like Adam, Noah consumes too much, this time of the fruit of the vine, gets drunk and is assaulted by his son Ham. This seems to be a rerun of the fall and intimates the need for a better Adam to save mankind from being engulfed in another wave of sin and violence.

Reading Gen 1–11 as a whole rather than as an anthology of separate tales thus gives a much richer picture of its interests. But though a connected reading gives a picture of a developing progression, does this make it history? It all depends on what we understand by history. Sparks speaks of "literal history" or an "accurate account of what actually took place" (p. 114). If something is to be described as history, "the author's representation [must be] accurate and successful" (p. 114). The story in Gen 2–3 is not "historical in the strict sense of the word" (p. 126). It is not strictly factual. The Cain and Abel story is a "tale," that is a "short fictional narrative" (p. 130). He holds that the biblical authors did not intend to write completely historically reliable narratives (p. 138).

I think it would have been helpful to have had more reflection on the nature of history. On the one hand, history refers to a sequence of events in a period of time. On the other hand, history is a human account of past events. And it is easy to confuse the two definitions. When we ask whether Gen 1–11 is historical we are asking whether it is describing events from the past. But Sparks imports into his definition of history criteria such as accuracy and factuality. He would appear to believe that accounts of the past can be objective and unbiased and that only accounts with these characteristics count as history. He seems to subscribe to von Ranke's goal of historiography: to describe the past *wie es eigentlich gewesen* ("as it actually was"). But in fact, we never have bare facts uninterpreted. All history is based on human testimony, which in the process of observation and then retelling past events interprets them.

Even if there is no explicit interpretation in a report, just the process of choosing which events to report introduces subjectivity and bias. Just think about television news reports. There is therefore no absolutely exhaustive record of the past, just a variety of testimonies, which later historians combine into their own accounts. These in turn reflect their own interests and biases. This is not to say that all accounts of the past are inaccurate or fictional, but that they do inevitably reflect the historian's own standpoint, and this might not be the same as ours.

I would therefore dispute Sparks' contention that inaccuracies in an account of the past means it is fiction, not history. As Sternberg pointed out,[88] whether an account of the past is to be classified as history depends on the writer's intention, not whether he was always accurate. Thus, something which we might classify as a tale or a myth might be regarded by its teller as history.

---

88. Sternberg, *The Poetics of Biblical Narrative*, 23–34.

WE DISAGREE. WHAT NOW?

"But the universe to the eye of the human understanding is framed like a labyrinth; presenting as it does on every side so many ambiguities of way, so many deceitful resemblances of objects and signs, natures so irregular in their lines, and so knotted and entangled."

Francis Bacon, *The Great Instauration*

"We live in a changing reality to which we try to adapt ourselves like seaweed bending under the pressure of water."

Giuseppe di Lampedusa, *The Leopard*

What do we do with a book like this? A book in which three expert scholars explain their differing perspectives in fairly lengthy essays and then offer critiques of each other pointing out supposed faults of greater or lesser degree in the other positions. One of the goals of this book is to help us understand the relationship between Gen 1–11 and history. If these experts are not able to agree on this topic, how is it possible for us to arrive at a firm conclusion regarding the Bible's beginning? The lack of census within this book can teach us something very important about the Christian life.

Agreement and Disagreement within a Lack of Consensus

The three contributors disagree with one another, at some points quite profoundly. Professor Hoffmeier believes that theology begins from the foundational understanding that the events recorded in Gen 1–11 really happened and that Israelite scribes did not borrow from Mesopotamian or Egyptian myths but were writing in opposition to them. The Israelite scribes corrected the misunderstandings and mythologies of their day with an authoritative and historically accurate account. Professor Wenham believes that there is a core of historical reality in Gen 1–11 but that the telling that we have is like an impressionist painting—we can only make out vague outlines of what really took place. Professor Sparks thinks that writers of the Bible employed standard forms of ancient historiography whose primary intent was not to precisely relay events that occurred in space and time. These scribes emplotted a theological story that reveals deep insights into the character and nature of God.

Even though they disagree with one another concerning the genre of the Bible's beginning, the contributors firmly agree that Gen 1–11 speaks truly about God. Hoffmeier sees this communication as straightforward historical narrative; Wenham understands it as more or less historical on the macro level; while Sparks believes that God communicates theological truths through certain accounts that did not actually happen in space and time.[1]

Reviewing their agreements is heartening but only to a certain extent. Eventually their commonalities highlight more profoundly their radical divergences. For instance, did the stories in Genesis really happen? Hoffmeier says yes, Wenham says sort of, and Sparks says probably not. Also, who even wrote Genesis? Hoffmeier seems to think the historical Moses did, Wenham believes that a series of authors wrote sections that were edited together into what is now Genesis, and Sparks agrees with Wenham that multiple authors wrote Genesis but he goes with a slightly different reconstruction of the sequence of when these chunks were written and edited. Now that we realize ever more deeply the range of conflicting interpretations regarding Gen 1–11—we can't even agree on who wrote Gen 1–11 much less if it happened or not—how should we respond?

Complexities of Interpretation

We don't read Gen 1–11 in the same ways as the early church mothers and fathers. For the most part, they were interested in reading Genesis allegorically, that is, symbolically. By and large, we don't approach the Bible that way. Biblical interpreters of the early church were not overly

---

1. Sparks did not make this connection but reading his essay made me think of Sarah Gorham's observation that "Artists prevaricate in order to tell the truth" (*Study in Perfect* [Athens, GA: University of Georgia Press, 2014], 66). In this sense, the writers of Genesis were literary artists who told the truth about God through stories that did not actually take place. Much like Jesus did through his parables.

concerned with whether Gen 1–11 was historical. They assumed that Scripture was true but they primarily thought of this through moral and theological categories rather than historical or scientific paradigms.[2] In contrast, we live in a technological age. It is only natural that we would look at Scripture from that perspective and have questions relating to its genre and whether the primeval history matches up with historical reconstructions from astro-physicists, genetic biologists, and historians of the ancient Near East. Furthermore, it would take around a millennium and a half after the biblical matriarchs and patriarchs for the scholarship of Hermann Gunkel to make genre an area of particular study.

But even more strikingly, we don't read the beginning of Scripture like those of scarcely a hundred and fifty years ago. Rarely did anyone in the early 19th century think of parts of Gen 1–11 as having an anti-Mesopotamian component because most Mesopotamian texts had not yet been discovered. But all of our contributors agree that Israelite scribes did engage with other ancient Near Eastern myths and tropes and this understanding figures largely within their interpretations.

Our goal should not be to recover the thought patterns of the saints of the past. The ancients and modernists had their questions and we have ours. There is some overlap between us as we share the commonalities of human experience but almost every facet of our lives in contemporary Western society is unfathomably different from theirs.[3] It is only natural, and even unavoidable, that our approaches to Gen 1–11 would be different. The saints of old—people like Augustine and Aquinas, Luther and Calvin—understood this about themselves. They were bold, revolutionary, and creative theologians that pushed their generations to think in new ways. They also recognized that they were capable of error and that later generations would need to correct them.

---

2. Peter C. Bouteneff, *Beginnings: Ancient Christian Readings of the Biblical Creation Narratives* (Grand Rapids: Baker Academic, 2008), 169–83.

3. This is seen even at one of the most basic levels of the human experience—the conceptual environment surrounding human perception of the divine. Charles Taylor highlights the tectonic shift that has happened in this regard with his question that framed his magnum opus, *A Secular Age*: "[W]hy was it virtually impossible not to believe in God in, say, 1500 in our Western society [not to mention Southwest Asian society in 500 BC!], while in 2000 many of us find this not only easy, but even inescapable?" (Cambridge, MA: Belknap Press, 2007), 25.

Augustine was very explicit that one should be open to changing one's mind when it comes to the book of Genesis: "[I]n matters that are obscure and far beyond our vision ... we should not rush in headlong and so firmly take our stand on one side that, if further progress in the search of truth justly undermines this position, we too fall with it. That would be to battle not for the teaching of Holy Scripture but for our own, wishing its teaching to conform to ours, whereas we ought to wish ours to conform to that of Sacred Scripture."[4] The Bible, like every other text, is not self-interpreting.[5] Augustine, along with those mentioned above, realized that humans construct interpretations from Scripture and these can be, and often are, in error. In his view, we should attempt to conform ourselves ever closer to Scripture, not to human constructions derived from Scripture.

Readers have an active role in forming the meanings and understandings that they embrace. The questions they ask of a writing, the ways in which they formulate synthetic conclusions, the methods they employ, the interpretive frameworks they bring, and even their emotional states and personal histories affect how they construct interpretations.[6] The emotional needs of readers may be the most overlooked shaper of interpretive outcomes because they often work on a subconscious level. And as Roger Scruton observed, in many cases emotional needs precede rational arguments and shape theological conclusions in advance.[7] Often times the conclusions we draw from the Bible have more to do with our emotional disposition—our fears and wants—than they do about the data that is in front of us. This is true when we read Gen 1–11 and this is one of the reasons why Christians often disagree over matters of Bible and theology. We bring different emotional needs to these debates.

It is true that we can never separate our cognitive selves from our emotional selves and that emotion often drives our logic, but rational

---

4. St. Augustine, *The Literal Meaning of Genesis* (trans. John Hammond Taylor, S.J.; 2 vols.; New York: Newman Press, 1982), 1:41.

5. Not only are texts not self-interpreting but words are imprecise and inherently ambiguous. Bruce Fink, *A Clinical Introduction to Lacanian Psychoanalysis: Theory and Technique* (Cambridge, MA: Harvard University Press, 1997), 22–27. All the more so when we communicate across time and culture.

6. Wolfgang Iser, *The Act of Reading: A Theory of Aesthetic Response* (Baltimore: Johns Hopkins University Press, 1978), 3–50.

7. Roger Scruton, *The Soul of the World* (Princeton: Princeton University Press, 2014), 1.

forces also cause diverse interpretations. For one thing, we have far more data now than did interpreters of the past. Archaeological discoveries, newly found cognate texts, and advances in literary theories, methods, memory studies and a host of other areas have forever changed the way we approach the task of understanding the Bible. There is no way to recover the reading experience of pre-modern interpreters who had no knowledge of formalized genre studies or the Gilgamesh and Atrahasis epics. They read the primeval history and understood it as best they could with their own limitations and insights and within their own context. We attempt to do the same within a radically different culture, with substantially more tools at our disposal, and from within a completely different philosophical and religious ecosystem.[8]

As time goes on, the task of reading the Bible will continue to change as additional ancient texts are found, methods of historical study are refined, and people approach Scripture with different questions and wants. This process of constantly revisiting and reevaluating biblical interpretation in light of new insights and contexts is something we *must* do if the Christian faith is to retain any form of intellectual coherence and attractiveness. As Elizabeth Johnson said, "To be plausible to any generation, Christian faith must express itself in ways consistent with the understanding of the world available at the time."[9] As we express Christian faith in new ways and interpret the Bible in light of new data, how much weight do we give to traditional understandings? The answer to this question produces different conclusions.

Charity, the Great Token

This is not to say that questions of genre and historicity are unimportant for the study of the book of Genesis. These are topics that concern many within the contemporary church and, accordingly, we should think deeply about them. In doing so, it is vitally important that we should take care to not let these issues become impediments to Christian unity.

---

8. For the latter, see Charles Taylor, *A Secular Age*, particularly pages 505–36.

9. Elizabeth Johnson, *Ask the Beasts: Darwin and the God of Love* (London: Bloomsbury, 2014), 9. Ernst Käsemann expressed this in a similar and, perhaps, more memorable way: "Christianity does not live from canned goods, especially not from such as are no longer edible and digestible" ("What 'To Believe' Means in the Evangelical Sense," in *On Being a Disciple of the Crucified Nazarene* [ed. Rudolf Landau; trans. Roy A. Harrisville; Grand Rapids: Eerdmans, 2010], 162).

Christians have a very long and deeply troubling history of division, rancor, exclusion, and fratricide over a myriad of issues, including the ways in which Gen 1–11 is understood. The root of these conflicts — whether they split churches, get seminary professors fired, or even lead to bloodshed — is a lack of charity.[10]

Determining the genre of Gen 1–11 and its proper interpretation is an extremely difficult task. To do it competently, one must be able to read Genesis in Hebrew and Greek, have a knowledge of the history of its interpretation, be acquainted with critical methods and conclusions, understand the various theories of historiography and the ways in which ancient authors composed narratives of the past, be able to compare Gen 1–11 with cognate texts, and so on. No one scholar is an expert in all of these areas but he or she must be familiar enough with each of them to skillfully synthesize their results into an overarching determination. This is no easy feat to be sure. And, as we have seen, supremely capable interpreters often arrive at very different conclusions.

Each of the contributors to this volume is a respected and senior scholar of biblical studies. Each of the contributors wrote their essays with deep insight and expertise that came from a lifetime of study. And all of the contributors share a concern that their work benefit the theological understanding and practice of the church. Nonetheless, each contributor offered different conclusions regarding the genre of Gen 1–11. This should give all of us who read their essays a healthy dose of humility and an appreciation for the complexities involved in this topic. If they cannot come to a consensus, this must be a thorny question indeed. Even more importantly, this fact should join Christian readers together even more deeply and make us all the more reticent to fracture the body of Christ when we have disagreements regarding issues such as this.

Let me make what might strike you as a startling claim. Actually, I'm not the one making it — I am repeating what St. Augustine has said: avoiding errors is not the primary task of interpretation.[11] In other words, when we are reading Scripture, our primary goal should not be

---

10. Ephraim Radner, *A Brutal Unity: The Spiritual Politics of the Christian Church* (Waco: Baylor University Press, 2012), 88.

11. Alan Jacobs, *A Theology of Reading: The Hermeneutics of Love* (Boulder, CO: Westview, 2001), 14–17.

to prevent ourselves from making a hermeneutical mistake. To put it differently, the thing we want most from our reading of the Bible should not be to attain its correct interpretation. Augustine was not saying that correctly understanding Scripture is unimportant. Arriving at proper interpretations was important for him but more paramount within the act of Christian reading is for the reader to interact with Scripture in a way that builds up charity. Augustine said: "[I]f he is deceived in an interpretation that builds up charity, which is the end of the commandments, he is deceived in the same way as a man who leaves a road by mistake but passes through a field to the same place toward which the road itself leads."[12] For Augustine, charity is what God most wants to foster, not correctness of belief. In his understanding, charity was such an essential component of Christian devotion that he said this within a sermon on 1 John: "But there is nothing to distinguish the sons of God from the sons of the devil, save charity. They that have charity, are born of God: they that have not charity are not. There is the great token, the great dividing mark."[13]

One might rejoin Augustine with Paul's desire that the church be united in "one mind" (Romans 15:6) and, accordingly, argue that uniformity of belief and correct interpretation are marks of the true church and are the goals for which we should aim. However, Ephraim Radner points out that in Romans 15 Paul links this one mindedness with "contributing to the needs of the saints," being "hospitable," "blessing one's persecutors," "rejoicing with those who rejoice and weeping with those who weep," and not being "haughty" or "conceited." In other words, Paul does not mean that Christians have one mind when they are united together in uniform doctrinal understanding and biblical interpretation. On the contrary, "Agreement is bound to *a way of living with one another* that is rooted in the heart or form of Christ Jesus and that grows out of a certain bondedness whereby deference is made to others."[14] Christians are united together in a way of life that points toward Christ. Of course, this implies that we share in common a few bedrock ideas (such as, who

---

12. St. Augustine, *On Christian Doctrine* (trans. D. W. Robertson, Jr; Indianapolis: Bobbs-Merrill, 1958), 31.

13. St. Augustine, "Fifth Homily on 1 John," in *Augustine: Later Works* (ed. and trans. John Burnaby; Philadelphia: Westminster Press, 1955), 298.

14. Radner, *A Brutal Unity*, 175, emphasis added.

is Jesus?), but Paul sees this one-mindedness as an interconnected way of life and not as unitary belief structure. This way of life is centered around deference to others, or, as Augustine may have put it, charity.

Christians are not a people who should fracture easily, particularly over the highly complex issues that we confront in Gen 1–11. Where there are areas of disagreement we must take pains to extend charity and deference to others, to recognize our own limitations, have patience with one another even as we work for change, and also rejoice in our agreement on the fundamental characteristics of the Christian faith. In Christian understanding, regardless of whether the events of the primeval history happened or not (or happened in the ways they are described), Gen 1–11 ultimately points toward the Christ in which Christians are rooted together and the person whom they are called to emulate.[15] This shared way of living with one another not only unites us together when we disagree over the genre of Gen 1–11 but it also unites us together with Christians of all times and places—Christians who had tremendously different outlooks on their faith than we do today. This way of life unites us with the likes of Augustine and Charles Wesley and Catherine of Sienna and Teresa of Calcutta. But this way of life also unites us with Origen who, along with being one of the church's greatest apologists and influencer of early trinitarian formulations, also denied the resurrection of the body and was denounced as a heretic by the Fifth Ecumenical Council in AD 553.[16] This way of life unites us to Martin Luther in spite of his, at times, virulently anti-semitic rants.[17] And it unites us to the Anglican Church that profited from directly owning and managing slaves on the Codrington plantation where punishments for slaves in the West Indies included being pinned to the ground and slowly burned from heel to head for rebellious behavior and for lesser crimes, castration and feet chopped in half.[18] Before we start

---

15. Richard B. Hays, *Reading Backwards: Figural Christology and the Fourfold Gospel Witness* (Waco: Baylor University Press, 2014).

16. Origen, "The Anathemas Against Origen," in *Nicene and Post-Nicene Fathers*, Series 2 (ed. Philip Schaff; 14 vols.; Peabody, MA: Hendrickson, 1994), 14:1885.

17. Eric W. Gritsch, *Martin Luther's Anti-Semitism: Against His Better Judgment* (Grand Rapids: Eerdmans, 2012).

18. On the Anglican Church's role in the Codrington plantation see Noel Leo Erskine, *Plantation Church: How African American Religion Was Born in Caribbean Slavery* (Oxford: Oxford University Press, 2014), 119. For a discussion of the punishments of slaves in the West

withholding charity from our brothers and sisters because they embrace a different idea regarding Genesis we would do well to contemplate the fact that if Origin, Luther, and the Anglican Church could stray so far, it is almost certain that generations from now Christians will look back on our ethics and beliefs with a mixture of horror and amusement. This should cause us to extend charity most generously to those with whom we disagree, particularly when it comes to topics as challenging as the genre of Gen 1–11.

Let us discuss matters such as the genre of Gen 1–11 and debate them vigorously if we desire. But if Christians are united together with the people and organizations that committed moral atrocities and who believed twisted and aberrant theologies, then how we regard Gen 1–11 should not come between us. May our God forgive us if this topic and even this book spur division in place of unity and strife instead of love.

Indies see Andro Linklater, *Owning the Earth: The Transforming History of Land Ownership* (New York: Bloomsbury, 2013), 264.

SCRIPTURE INDEX

Genesis

1 . . . . .29, 81, 123, 128, 144
1–11 . . .19–21, 23–72, 73–109, 110–54, 155–63
1–15 . . .31, 40, 50, 77, 78, 79, 89, 92
1–16 40
1–55 31
1:1 79
1:1–2 79
1:1–2:3 . . . .52, 73, 78, 79, 80
1:1–2:14 36
1:1–6:8 35–36
1:1–11:9 35
1:2 153
1:7 40
1:9 138
1:26–27 145
1:26–28 141
1:28 82
2 . . . . . . .34, 123, 144, 145
2–3 . . . .123, 124, 127, 145, 146, 154
2–4 77
2–9 92
2–11 73
2:1 123
2:1–3 79
2:4 . . . . .29, 61, 78, 79, 81
2:4–3:24 52
2:4–4:26 77
2:4–11:9 81
2:4–11:32 78
2:4b–4:26 29
2:7 141
2:8–3:24 32
2:10–14 . . . .32–33, 59
2:15 41

2:15–24 36
2:17 124
2:18 82
2:23 . . . . 69, 73
2:24 82
2:32–33 59
3 . . . . .82, 83, 101, 145
3:6 90
3:14–19 73
3:17 77
3:22 . . . . 90, 91
3:22–24 94
3:24 52
4 . . . . . . 118, 119, 120, 121, 122, 130, 141, 150, 152
4:1–16 36
4:1–26 52
4:8 37
4:12 134
4:16 52
4:17–5:32 36
4:17–18 152
4:17–22 . . . . 73, 74
4:17–24 75
4:19–24 152
4:20–22 76
4:23 119
4:23–24 . . . . 37, 73
4:24 . . . . 76, 92
4:25–26 . . . . 73, 75
4:26 35
5 . . . . . . 35, 65, 73, 77, 85, 86, 88, 118, 119, 120, 121, 127, 150, 152
5:1 61
5:1–6:8 29
5:1–32 . . .73, 75, 76, 77
5:1b–2 145
5:2 29
5:2–9:29 52

5:6–8 119
5:24 76
5:25–27 78
5:29 77
5:32 78
6 . . . . 36, 101
6–9 . . . 43, 77, 93, 94, 131, 153
6:1–4 . . .20, 35, 36, 37, 60, 67, 68, 88
6:1–8 . . . . . . 35, 36, 37
6:2 90
6:3 90
6:4 . . . . 38, 124
6:5 . . . . 41, 88, 92
6:5–8 . . . . . . 37, 88, 91
6:6–7 78
6:9 . . . . .36, 37, 62, 91, 153
6:9–9:2 36
6:9–9:26 . . . . . . 20, 29
6:9–9:28 49
6:9–9:29 . . . . . 77, 91
6:9–11:9 . . . . . . 36, 37
6:9–17 48
6:9a 29
6:10–7:24 50
6:10a, b 50
6:11 94
6:14–21 50
7:1 153
7:1–3 50
7:1–10 136
7:4–5 50
7:7–10 50
7:7b–18 50
7:11 93
7:11–13 136
7:11–16 50
7:17a 50
7:19–24 50
8:1 . . . . 50, 53, 92, 153
8:2–19 50

164

8:3–5.............50
8:6–12.............45
8:6a, b.............50
8:7–9.............50
8:10–13.............50
8:14.............93
8:15–16.............50
8:20–22.............92
8:21.............53
8:22.............92
9.............101
9:1–4.............50
9:1–7.............134
9:3–17.............36
9:6.............92, 134
9:6b.............145
9:8–10.............50
9:11.............93
9:11–17.............50
9:18–27.............36
9:18a, b.............50
9:19.............50
9:20–27.............107
9:22–27.............91
9:25.............116
9:26.............119
9:28.............78
9:28–29.............78
10.....36, 53, 55, 65,
69, 73, 75, 76, 94,
115, 118, 121, 122
10:1.......29, 53, 55
10:1–11:9.........29
10:2–7.............77
10:4.............55
10:7.............121
10:10.........53, 56
10:11.............121
10:13–14.........77
10:15.............108
10:20.............55
10:22.............121
10:29.............121
10:31.............55
11.....55, 57, 65, 69,
73, 85, 86, 101,
118, 121, 127

11:1.........56, 69
11:1–9.....20, 36, 37,
55, 94
11:4.............94
11:7.............56
11:9.........56, 135
11:10–26...29, 76, 91
11:10–32......55, 73
11:10a.............29
11:26.........75, 78
11:26–32.............37
11:27–25:11...29, 77
11:27–32.........25
11:27a.............29
11:32.............78
12–50.....26, 77, 85
12:1–3.............25
18–19.............94
19.............91
21:5.............78
23.............108
25:7.............78
25:12.........29, 61
25:12–18......29, 77
25:19–20.........78
25:19–35:29...29, 77
25:19a.............29
26.............29
29:14.............82
35:28–29.........78
36:1.........29, 61
36:1–8.............29
36:1–37:1.........77
36:9.........29, 77
36:9–42.............29
37:1–50:26.......29
37:2.........29, 78
37:2–50:26.......77
50:22–26.........78

Exodus
2:3.............43
2:5.............43

Leviticus
16.............128
18.............91

Numbers
3:1.............29
13.............38
13:33.........38, 91

Judges
1:11.............38

Ruth
4:18.............29

1 Samuel
16:14.............39
16:18.............38
17:51.............38

2 Samuel
11.............114

1 Kings
1:33.............34
22:22.............39
38.............34
45.............34

2 Kings
19:9.............34

1 Chronicles
1:29.............29
16:30b.............14

2 Chronicles
32:30.............34

Esther
1:1.............34

Job
1:6.........39, 89
2:1.............89
3:8.............28
38:7.............144
41:1.............28

Psalms
2:7.............89
74:14.............28
78:4, 7.........58

95:3, 4 89
97:7, 9 89
104:26 28
121:4 53
137:1, 4 54

Isaiah
18:1 34
20:3 34
27:1 28
51:9 28

Ezekiel
18:20 116
28. 125
29:10 34
32:2 28
47:12 145

Daniel
1:1–6 54
3:18 54

Luke
3:23–38 145

John
5:39–40 116
9:2–3 116

Acts
17:32 142

Romans
3:23 126
15:6 161

1 Corinthians
1:23 142

15:16–19 143
15:22 145
15:45 145

Hebrews
11. 149
11:1–3 125

2 Peter
2:4 89

Jude
1:14 115
6. 89
7. 89

Revelation
22:1–2 145

SUBJECT INDEX

Adapa Myth, 63, 66, 125
agreement and interpretation, 153–63
Alter, Robert, 35, 48–49, 70, 151
ancient historiography, 110–54
  believers/unbelievers, 110, 140–45
  creation account, 123–24, 127–28, 144–45
  Edenic garden, 111, 125, 141, 144–45
  genealogies and, 118–22
  Genesis 1–11 as, 20, 110–54
  genre and, 112–115, 130–31
  history of humanity, 111, 143
  human words, 116–17
  legends, 129–36
  myths, 122–29
  paradise/fall story, 123–27, 144–45, 150
  primeval history, 117–18
  science and, 110–12, 142–45
  tales, 129–36
  tree of life, 124–25, 141, 145
  Word of God, 115–16
Anthologist, 60, 136–37, 146, 151–53
Antiquarian, 60, 119–22, 126–27, 130–39, 145–46, 151
Apologist, 60, 121, 127–29, 131–38, 146, 151–52, 162
Aquinas, St. Thomas, 110, 140, 142, 157
ark. See also flood stories
  building, 45, 47–48, 132–33
  commands for, 132, 153
  interpretation of, 20, 41–54, 60, 136
  purpose of, 45, 86–88, 132
  symbolic numbers and, 132–33
"Ark tablet," 47–48
Aronofsky, Darren, 41
Assyrian king lists, 31, 65

atheism, 75
Atrahasis Epic, 44, 46, 51–52, 66, 85–86, 92, 117, 153, 159
Augustine, 40, 110, 140, 157–62
Averbeck, Richard, 28, 30

Babylonian king list, 152
Bacon, Francis, 155
Basilica of Santa Croce, 13
believers/unbelievers, 110, 140–45
biblical characters, 25–27, 35–41
biblical interpretations, 15–21, 24, 159–61
biblical scholarship, 25–27, 35–48, 63, 69, 82–85, 143, 146
biblical tradition, 48–53
"Book of the Cow of Heaven, The," 43
Bultmann, Rudolf, 143
Bunyan, Paul, 39

Cain and Abel story, 84, 130–31, 134, 141, 154
Calvin, John, 21, 39–40, 157
Carroll, Lewis, 13
Cassuto, Umberto, 39, 40, 49, 55
charity, 159–63
Clement of Alexandria, 39
Clines, David, 24–25, 146
Coats, George, 56
cognitive environment, 74
conclusion, 155–63
creation, account of, 17, 79–86, 123–24, 127–28, 144–45
creation, of humans, 46–47, 52, 80–86, 92, 128
Creation Epic, 94. See also Enuma Elish
Crowe, Russell, 41
cuneiform tablets, 42, 47. See also tablets

"daughters of man," 35–38, 67, 88–91
Delitzsch, Franz, 29
"Destruction of Mankind," 43
disagreement and interpretation, 153–63
dogmatism, 150, 151
Dozeman, Thomas, 70
Driver, S. R., 30, 48

Edenic garden, 66–67, 111, 125, 141, 144–45. *See also* garden of Eden
Ehrman, Bart, 143
el-Baz, Farouk, 34
Eliade, Mircea, 27
emic interpretation, 73–75, 88, 92, 98
Enns, Peter, 27
Enuma Elish, 28, 63, 66, 94, 123, 127–28
Epic of Creation, 94. *See also Enuma Elish*
"Eridu Genesis, The," 86–87, 93, 109, 117
etic interpretation, 73–75, 98
evolution, 102, 144

"faded myth," 80, 84. *See also* myths
fall story, 123–27, 144–45, 150
"fallen" beings, 38–39, 67–68
family histories, 28–32, 49, 53, 91–92. *See also* genealogies
Finkel, Irving, 44, 47–49, 52, 55
flood stories
    ark and, 41–54, 60, 86–88, 91–93, 132–33, 136, 153
    chronology in, 38, 85–86, 95–96, 132, 137
    flood traditions and, 27, 41–56, 132–34
    heroes in, 38–46, 53, 60–61, 65, 120, 132–34, 139
    interpretation of, 20, 32, 36–38, 41–54, 60
    myths and, 27, 104–08
    parallels to, 85–86, 91–93

primeval history and, 130–35
representation and, 114–15
responses on, 60–65, 68–69
terminology in, 76–78
flood traditions, 27, 41–56, 132–33
"Folly of Babel," 95

Galilei, Galileo, 13–16, 20, 110
garden of Eden
    geographical details of, 32–35, 66–67
    interpretation of, 81–82
    life and, 81–83
    protohistory and, 43, 81–83, 95
    responses on, 59–62
    sin and, 81–82
    stories of, 32–33, 73, 82–85, 95, 123–25, 131, 144–45
    tree of life and, 124–25, 141, 145
genealogies
    expanded genealogies, 78–85, 95–98, 106–07
    family histories and, 28–32, 49, 53, 91–92
    features of, 76–78, 118
    function of, 75–78
    in Genesis 1–11, 28–32, 49, 53, 61–65, 73–86, 91–92, 95–98, 106–07, 118–22
    historiography and, 118–22
    importance of, 31–32, 59–60
    king lists and, 30–31, 73, 106–07, 121, 129, 137
    linear genealogies, 65, 75–76, 106, 118–22
    protohistory and, 75–85
    segmented genealogies, 75–76, 106, 118–22
general representation, 102, 114–15
Genesis 1–11
    as ancient historiography, 20, 110–54
    anthologist in, 60, 136–37, 146, 151–53
    chronology in, 38, 85–88, 93–99, 107, 118–21, 132, 137

family histories in, 28–32, 49, 53,
        91–92
genealogies in, 28–32, 49, 53,
        61–65, 73–86, 91–92,
        95–98, 106–07, 118–22
genre identification and, 20, 106
genre interpretations and, 19–21,
        24
genre of, 20–21, 25–32, 62,
        73–79, 101–02
geographical clues in, 20, 58
geographical details in, 32–35,
        45–46, 52–53, 58–60,
        66–67, 98
historicity of, 41–42, 58–59, 64,
        67, 71–72, 84, 101–04,
        108, 138, 143, 159–60
as historiography, 110–54
as history, 20, 23–72
as "human words," 116–17
implications of, 20
interpretation of, 15–21, 24, 110,
        159–61
labels and, 104–109, 112,
        129–30
legends in, 25–26, 129–36
myths in, 122–29
overview of, 24–25
parallels to, 85–95
as primeval history, 84, 117–18
as protohistory, 20, 73–109
recovering message of, 74–75,
        95–97
redemption in, 23
science and, 110–12
tales in, 129–36
as theology, 20, 23–72
as Word of God, 35–41, 103–05,
        111, 115–17
genre
    categories of, 112–14
    cultural differences and, 19–20
    definition of, 112
    family histories and, 28–32
    of Genesis 1–11, 20–21, 25–32,
        62, 73–79, 101–02
    historicity and, 101, 159

history and, 145–49
identification of, 20, 109
implications of, 20–21
interpretation of, 19–21, 24
legend and, 25–26
literature and, 112–14, 145–49
musings on, 112–15, 130–31
myth and, 26–28, 82–85
protohistory and, 82–85
sensitivity to, 20–21
study of, 13–21
thoughts on, 112–15, 130–31
types of, 20–21
genre identification, 20, 109
genre interpretations, 19–21, 24
geographical clues, 20, 58
geographical details, 32–35, 45–46,
        52–53, 58–60, 66–67, 98
George, Andrew, 27
Gilgamesh Epic, 38, 42, 44–48,
        51–52, 86, 90–92, 125, 153,
        159
God
    creation and, 79–86, 123–24,
        127–28
    knowledge of, 21
    sons of, 35–41, 67, 88–91
    Word of, 35–41, 103–05, 111,
        115–17
Gunkel, Hermann, 17–18, 25–26,
        48, 55–56, 80, 84, 148, 157
Güterbock, Hans, 56

Hebrew tradition, 48–53, 56–57
Hendel, Ronald S., 68
Hess, Richard, 31
historical realities, 91, 95, 155
historical representation, 64, 67, 102,
        114
historiography. See ancient histori-
        ography
history and theology, 23–72
    family histories and, 28–32
    flood stories, 41–57
    garden of Eden and, 32–35
    Genesis 1–11 as, 20, 23–72
    genre and, 145–49

geographical details in, 32–35, 45–46, 52–53, 58–60, 66
of humanity, 111, 143
legend and, 25–26
literary overview, 24–25
literature and, 145–49
myths, 25–28
responses on, 59–72
Hoffmeier, James K.
on history and theology, 20, 23, 155–56
responses by, 98–100, 140–49
responses to, 59–72, 108–09, 150–51
human evolution, 102, 144
"human words," 116–17

interpretation
agreement and, 153–63
biblical interpretations, 15–21, 24, 159–61
complexities of, 110, 156–59
disagreement and, 153–63
emic interpretation, 73–75, 88, 92, 98
etic interpretation, 73–75, 98
of Genesis 1–11, 15–21, 24, 110
genre interpretations, 19–21, 24
protohistory and, 73–75, 88, 92, 98
purpose of, 160–61
science and, 142–45
scripture and, 142–45

Jacobsen, Thorkild, 86, 93
Jesus
death of, 142
incarnation of, 142
parables of, 62, 64, 114, 156
resurrection of, 114, 142–43, 162
as way of life, 161–62
Jewish tradition, 59
John Paul II, Pope, 14
Johnson, Elizabeth, 159

Keil, C. F., 29
Kikawada, Isaac M., 51–52, 70–71

king lists
Assyrian king lists, 31, 65
Babylonian king list, 152
genealogies and, 30–31, 73, 106–07, 121, 129, 137
Mesopotamian king lists, 118, 120–21, 129, 152
Sumerian king lists, 17, 38, 46, 109, 117
Kitchen, Kenneth, 51
Kramer, Samuel Noah, 57

labels, 104–109, 112, 129–30
Lambert, W. G., 44, 46
Lampedusa, Giuseppe di, 155
legends
in ancient historiography and, 129–36
biblical characters and, 25–27, 35–41
category of, 26
in Genesis 1–11, 25–26, 129–36
genre and, 25–26
theology and, 25–26
Lewis, C. S., 64
linear genealogies, 65, 75–76, 106, 118–22. See also genealogies
"lists," 117–20, 152. See also king lists
literal history, 111, 126–27, 138, 141, 143, 154
literary categories, 23–27, 46, 71, 73, 79–85, 106–07, 112, 142, 147–48
literary pictures, 104–06
literary texts, 42
literary theories, 159
literary traditions, 43, 48, 54
literature
genre and, 112–14, 145–49
history and, 145–49
myths and, 26–28, 35, 41–43
Long, V. Philips, 99
Louis, Kenneth Gros, 35
Lowery, Daniel D., 76
Luther, Martin, 157, 162–63

Mesopotamian flood. *See also* flood
    stories
    flood traditions, 27, 41–56,
        132–34
    myths and, 27, 99, 146–49
    parallels to, 85–86
Mesopotamian king lists, 118,
    120–21, 129, 152
Mesopotamian myths, 27, 99,
    146–49
Mesopotamian texts, 85–95,
    99–100, 117–20, 157
Mesopotamian traditions, 27,
    41–56, 132–34
Millard, Alan, 31, 44, 46, 55
Miller, Johnny, 144
Milton, John, 23
monotheism, 54–55, 92, 129,
    132–34, 153
Muilenburg, James, 35
Museo Galileo, 13
mythical imagery, 14, 63–64
mytho-historical accounts, 87, 93, 96
myths
    acceptance of, 26–28
    in biblical scholarship, 25–27,
        35–41
    definition of, 27, 64
    "faded myth," 80, 84
    in Genesis 1–11, 122–29
    genre and, 26–28, 82–85
    imagery and, 14, 63–64
    literature and, 26–28, 35, 41–43
    Mesopotamian myths, 27, 99,
        146–49
    protohistory and, 80, 82–85
    rejection of, 82–84, 104–05
    theology and, 25–28

Nephilim story
    historiography and, 124, 131
    interpretation of, 20, 32, 36–40,
        58–59
    parallels to, 88–91
    primeval history and, 130–31
    responses on, 38–39, 59–60,
        67–68

Nicholson, E. W., 24
Noah, 41
nominalism, 104
numbers, symbolic, 79, 98, 120,
    132–33

Origen, 138, 162–63

parables, 62, 64, 114, 156
"Paradise Lost," 23
"Paradise Regained," 23
paradise/fall story, 123–27, 144–45,
    150
polytheism, 85, 92
postmodernism, 151
"priestly doctrine," 80, 84
primeval history, 84, 117–18,
    130–31, 135–36
protohistory, 73–109
    creation account, 79–86
    garden of Eden and, 73, 81–83,
        95
    genealogies and, 75–85
    Genesis 1–11 as, 20, 73–109
    genre and, 82–85
    interpretation and, 73–75, 88,
        92, 98
    literary categories, 73, 79–85,
        106–07
    Mesopotamian parallels, 85–95
    myth and, 80, 82–85
    responses on, 98–109
    sin and, 81–91, 96

Quinn, Arthur, 51–52, 70–71

Radner, Ephraim, 161
Ramesses II, 28
realism, 104
redemption story, 23
Redford, Donald, 30
Rendsburg, Gary, 36, 70, 71
Rendtorff, Rolf, 151
representation, general, 102, 114–15
representation, historical, 64, 67,
    102, 114

resurrection, 114, 142–43, 162
Römer, Thomas, 70
Roskop, Angela R., 13
Ryken, Leland, 35

Sarna, Nahum, 38, 40, 56
Sasson, Jack, 35, 70
Sauer, James, 34
Schmid, Konrad, 70
science
    Genesis 1–11 and, 110–12
    historiography and, 110–12,
        142–45
    interpretation and, 142–45
    scripture and, 142–45
Scruton, Roger, 158
segmented genealogies, 75–76, 106,
    118–22. *See also* genealogies
Septuagint, 38, 39
seven, multiples of, 79, 132–33
Shalmaneser V, 31
sin
    descriptions of, 82
    effects of, 81–82
    increase in, 91
    paradigm of, 82, 84–85
    protohistory and, 81–91, 96
    understanding of, 82, 88–89, 96,
        116, 124
Soden, John, 144
"sons of God/gods," 35–41, 67,
    88–91
Sparks, Kenton L.
    on ancient historiography, 20, 27,
        110, 156
    responses by, 63–71, 101–08
    responses to, 140–54
Speiser, E. A., 32
Sternberg, Meir, 62, 151, 154
sui generis, 73, 102, 117, 141–42
Sumerian king lists, 17, 38, 46, 65,
    86, 109, 117
Swift, Jonathan, 18
symbolic numbers, 79, 98, 120,
    132–33

"Table of Nations," 53, 55, 65,
    73–76, 88, 94, 115, 121–22
tablets, 42–44, 47–48, 74–75, 86
tales, 129–36
theology and history, 23–72
    family histories and, 28–32
    flood stories, 41–57
    garden of Eden and, 32–35
    Genesis 1–11 as, 20, 23–72
    geographical details in, 32–35,
        45–46, 52–53, 58–60, 66
    legend and, 25–26
    literary overview, 24–25
    myths, 25–28
    responses on, 59–72
tôlĕdôt formula, 29–32, 36, 49, 62,
    64
Torah, 40, 54–55
Tower of Babel
    interpretation of, 20, 32, 36–37,
        55–60, 81–82
    parallels to, 88–91, 94–97
    primeval history and, 130–31,
        135–36
    responses on, 60, 69, 150
traditions
    biblical tradition, 48–53
    flood traditions, 27, 41–56,
        130–33
    Hebrew tradition, 48–53, 56–57
    Jewish tradition, 59
    Mesopotamian traditions, 27,
        41–56, 132–34
tree of life, 23, 82, 90, 124–25, 141,
    145

Ussher, Archbishop, 59, 120

Van Seters, John, 146, 147
von Rad, Gerhard, 30, 32, 80, 84
von Ranke, Leopold, 154

Wall, Christopher, 21
Wellhausen, Julius, 24, 54, 146–47
Wenham, Gordon J.
    on protohistory, 20, 23, 31, 40,
        49–51, 63, 73, 155–56

responses by, 59–62, 150–54
responses to, 98–109
Westermann, Claus, 41, 73, 80, 84
Whybray, Norman, 150
Windschuttle, Keith, 148
Word of God, 35–41, 103–05, 111,
115–17